CELESTIAL FLAMES OF THE STARSEED ASCENSION

Harnessing the Cosmic Fire to
Ignite Soul Evolution

Carey Lee James

S.D.N Publishing

Copyright © 2024 S.D.N Publishing

All rights reserved

The characters and events portrayed in this book are fictitious. Any similarity to real persons, living or dead, is coincidental and not intended by the author.

No part of this book may be reproduced, or stored in a retrieval system, or transmitted in any form or by any means, electronic, mechanical, photocopying, recording, or otherwise, without express written permission of the publisher.

ISBN: 9798339117032

CONTENTS

Title Page
Copyright
General Disclaimer — 1
Awakening the Cosmic Flame — 3
The Soul's Journey Through Ascension — 24
Ascending Through the Dimensions — 47
Sacred Symbols and the Cosmic Language — 69
Meditation and Ritual for Ascension — 90
The Starseed Light Body Activation — 112
Collective Starseed Ascension — 133
Emotional Alchemy and Soul Healing — 155
Sacred Cosmic Relationships — 176
Galactic Wisdom and Cosmic Guides — 198
Ascension Tools and Practices — 220
Becoming a Cosmic Leader — 241
THE END — 263

GENERAL DISCLAIMER

This book is intended to provide general information to the reader on the topics covered. The author and publisher have made every effort to ensure that the information herein is accurate and up-to-date at the time of publication. However, they do not warrant or guarantee the accuracy, completeness, adequacy, or currency of the information contained in this book. The author and publisher expressly disclaim any liability or responsibility for any errors or omissions in the content herein.

The information, guidance, advice, tips, and suggestions provided in this book are not intended to replace professional advice or consultation. Readers are strongly encouraged to consult with an appropriate professional for specific advice tailored to their situation before making any decisions or taking any actions based on the content of this book.

The views and opinions expressed in this book are those of the author and do not necessarily reflect the official policy or position of any other agency, organization, employer or company.

The author and publisher are not responsible for any actions taken or not taken by the reader based on the information, advice, or suggestions provided in this book. The reader is solely responsible for their actions and the consequences thereof.

This book is not intended to be a source of legal, business, medical or psychological advice, and readers are cautioned to seek the services of a competent professional in these or other areas of expertise.

All product names, logos, and brands are property of their respective owners. All company, product and service names used in this book are for identification purposes only. Use of these names, logos, and brands does not imply endorsement.

Readers of this book are advised to do their own due diligence when it comes to making decisions and all information, products, services and advice that have been provided should be independently verified by your own qualified professionals.

By reading this book, you agree that the author and publisher are not responsible for your success or failure resulting from any information presented in this book.

AWAKENING THE COSMIC FLAME

The Celestial Origins of Starseeds

Throughout the vast expanse of the universe, there exists a profound mystery woven into the fabric of creation: the existence of Starseeds. These cosmic beings are not confined by the limitations of a single planet or a singular reality. Instead, they are scattered across galaxies, born with the divine purpose of igniting a higher spiritual evolution. Starseeds are the cosmic travelers, the ancient souls who have incarnated across multiple star systems before descending to Earth to assist in its ascension.

For many, the feeling of being a Starseed is a deep, inner knowing—a resonance with the stars that cannot be explained by earthly logic. This sensation often manifests as a yearning for something beyond the confines of our physical existence. Starseeds are believed to carry the genetic imprints and vibrational frequencies of their celestial origins, a cosmic flame that burns deep within their souls. As they awaken to their true purpose, this flame ignites, guiding them through the process of ascension.

The Purpose of Starseeds

The role of Starseeds in the grand cosmic design is both ancient and vital. Starseeds are considered volunteers, souls who have chosen to incarnate on Earth to assist in raising the planet's vibration and supporting the collective shift in consciousness. This task, often referred to as "the Great Awakening," is part of a universal process known as ascension. It involves elevating not only personal consciousness but also the collective energy of humanity and the Earth itself.

At the heart of this mission is the belief that Earth is moving from a lower vibrational density (commonly referred to as the third dimension, or 3D) to a higher one (the fifth dimension, or 5D). In this new reality, love, unity, and spiritual awareness become the dominant forces, replacing the fear-based consciousness that has long governed human existence. Starseeds are seen as critical players in facilitating this shift, as they bring with them the wisdom, energy, and light from their respective star systems.

Each Starseed has a unique mission, which may vary depending on their star lineage. Some Starseeds may focus on healing and raising the vibration of individuals, while others work on planetary healing, helping to stabilize Earth's energy grids and promote environmental harmony. Despite these differences in purpose, all Starseeds share a common goal: to assist humanity in remembering its divine origins and ascending to higher states of being.

The Cosmic Flame: A Catalyst for Awakening

At the core of the Starseed's mission is the concept of the Cosmic Flame. This flame is not a physical fire but a metaphysical energy that burns within the soul. It represents the purest essence of divine light, a spark of Source energy that connects all beings across the universe. For Starseeds, the Cosmic Flame is the catalyst for their spiritual awakening and the key to unlocking their full potential.

When a Starseed awakens, the Cosmic Flame within them begins to burn more brightly. This awakening is often accompanied by a deep sense of purpose and an overwhelming desire to understand their true nature. It may be triggered by a variety of experiences, such as a life-changing event, a spiritual awakening, or even a simple recognition of the soul's calling. For some, this process is gradual, while for others, it can happen suddenly, like a bolt of lightning that ignites their awareness.

The Cosmic Flame is more than just a symbol of spiritual power; it is a living energy that interacts with the Starseed's entire being. It cleanses the soul, purifies the mind, and awakens the dormant codes within their DNA—codes that contain the wisdom and knowledge of their star ancestors. This flame also serves as a bridge between the Starseed and their cosmic origins, allowing them to access higher realms of consciousness and receive guidance from their star families.

The Origins of Starseeds: Celestial Lineages

To fully understand the essence of Starseeds, it is important to explore their celestial lineages. Starseeds come from various star systems, each carrying the unique frequencies and characteristics of their cosmic home. Among the most commonly recognized star systems are the Pleiades, Sirius, Arcturus, Andromeda, and Orion. While each Starseed's lineage may differ, they all share a common thread: a deep connection to the stars and the divine mission to assist in the ascension of Earth.

- **Pleiadian Starseeds**: Known for their gentle, nurturing energy, Pleiadian Starseeds are often seen as healers and teachers. They carry the vibration of unconditional love and work to inspire peace, compassion, and unity on Earth. Pleiadians are highly connected to the heart chakra and emphasize emotional healing and the importance of spiritual community.
- **Sirius Starseeds**: Sirius, one of the brightest stars in the night sky, is home to a highly advanced and technologically evolved civilization. Sirius Starseeds often have a strong connection to water and the energy of the divine feminine. They are here to bring balance between technology and spirituality, guiding humanity toward a future where both are in harmony.
- **Arcturian Starseeds**: Arcturians are known as the spiritual guardians of the universe, and their Starseeds often possess a deep wisdom and a highly developed spiritual intellect. Arcturian Starseeds are here to guide the ascension process by providing spiritual knowledge and assisting in the development of new, advanced healing technologies.
- **Andromedan Starseeds**: Known for their free-spirited nature, Andromedan Starseeds are often focused on personal freedom and autonomy. They carry the energy of liberation and are here to help humanity break free from limiting belief systems and societal structures.
- **Orion Starseeds**: Orion Starseeds are warriors of light, often tasked with breaking down old paradigms and fighting for justice and truth. They are here to dismantle systems of control and help usher in a new

age of spiritual freedom and empowerment.

Each Starseed carries the energetic imprint of their star system, and this lineage influences their mission on Earth. However, regardless of their origin, all Starseeds share the same core purpose: to assist in the collective ascension of humanity.

Signs of a Starseed Awakening

The awakening process for a Starseed is a deeply personal and transformative experience. It often begins with a feeling of not quite belonging on Earth, as if something about the physical world does not fully align with their soul's essence. This sense of "otherness" can manifest as a longing for home—a place that feels distant yet familiar, often leading Starseeds to look to the stars for answers.

Common signs of a Starseed awakening include:

- A strong fascination with the cosmos and a feeling of connection to the stars.
- A sense of purpose or mission, even if it is not yet fully understood.
- Experiences of synchronicity and spiritual phenomena, such as vivid dreams, visions, or encounters with otherworldly beings.
- A growing interest in metaphysical subjects, such as energy healing, meditation, and ascension.
- A desire to serve humanity and contribute to the healing and transformation of the planet.

As Starseeds awaken to their true nature, they begin to remember their soul's mission and align with the energy of the Cosmic Flame. This flame acts as both a guide and a tool for their ascension, helping them to navigate the challenges of the physical world while staying connected to their higher purpose.

Embracing the Celestial Journey

The journey of a Starseed is one of profound transformation and spiritual evolution. It is a path that requires courage, resilience, and an unwavering commitment to the light. As the Cosmic Flame burns within, Starseeds are called to step into their power, embrace their divine mission, and assist in the ascension of humanity and the Earth.

For those who feel the pull of the stars, who sense the awakening of the flame within, the path ahead is one of discovery, healing, and expansion. You are not alone on this journey. The universe is vast, and your soul's mission is grand. Together, as Starseeds, we ignite the flames of ascension, lighting the way for a new age of spiritual awakening on Earth.

Understanding the Cosmic Fire's Role in Ascension

The journey of a Starseed is one that spans dimensions, lifetimes, and galaxies. But at the core of every Starseed's evolution is the Cosmic Flame—a universal force of pure divine energy that propels the soul toward ascension.

The Nature of the Cosmic Flame

The Cosmic Flame is not merely a metaphor; it is a living energy, an extension of Source itself. Often referred to as the divine spark, the Cosmic Flame resides within every soul but remains dormant until it is consciously awakened. This flame holds the blueprint of each Starseed's journey, encoded with the knowledge, wisdom, and frequencies from other star systems and dimensions. While it is present in all beings, Starseeds are uniquely attuned to its vibration, as their souls carry the celestial frequency that harmonizes with this fire.

In essence, the Cosmic Flame is the light of ascension, a guiding force that illuminates the path from spiritual slumber to full cosmic awakening. It serves as a bridge between the dense, material plane and the higher dimensions of consciousness. For Starseeds, this flame is the key to unlocking their higher abilities, including intuition, telepathy, and the capacity to channel divine wisdom. It is the catalyst for personal transformation and the fuel that powers the Starseed's mission to elevate humanity's consciousness.

The Cosmic Flame as a Tool for Transformation

At the heart of ascension lies transformation—the shedding of old energies, beliefs, and patterns that no longer serve the soul's highest good. This process, though often challenging, is necessary for the Starseed's evolution. The Cosmic Flame acts as a purifying agent, burning away lower vibrational energies and allowing the soul to rise into higher states of awareness.

When the Cosmic Flame is activated, it brings forth profound shifts on all levels of being: physical, emotional, mental, and spiritual. These changes may be subtle at first, manifesting as heightened intuition or an increased sense of empathy, but as the flame intensifies, the Starseed may experience a deeper connection to their soul's purpose and a clearer sense of direction.

This transformative fire also plays a crucial role in clearing karmic patterns. Many Starseeds carry karmic imprints from past lifetimes, not only from Earth but from other star systems as well. These imprints can manifest as unresolved fears, limiting beliefs, or repetitive cycles that block the soul's progress. By working with the Cosmic Flame, Starseeds can dissolve these energetic blockages, freeing themselves from the constraints of karma and aligning with the frequency of ascension.

Ascension and the Shift in Consciousness

Ascension, in its simplest form, is the process of raising one's consciousness from a lower state of awareness to a higher one. For Earth, this means moving from a 3D reality, governed by duality and separation, to a 5D consciousness, where unity, love, and oneness prevail. The Cosmic Flame plays an integral role in this shift, as it accelerates the evolution of the soul and enables Starseeds to embody higher dimensional frequencies.

When the Cosmic Flame is awakened within a Starseed, it ignites the process of ascension by activating dormant codes within their DNA. These codes, often referred to as ascension codes or star codes, contain the information and guidance necessary for the soul's evolution. As these codes are activated, the Starseed begins to resonate with higher frequencies, which leads to profound changes in perception, behavior, and spiritual understanding.

In the context of ascension, the Cosmic Flame can be likened to a lighthouse, guiding the soul through the stormy seas of transformation. It offers clarity and direction, helping Starseeds navigate the sometimes overwhelming process of spiritual awakening. As the flame grows stronger, it opens the doors to multidimensional awareness, allowing the Starseed to access higher realms of consciousness and interact with their galactic guides and star families.

The Role of the Cosmic Flame in Collective Ascension

While the Cosmic Flame serves as a personal tool for ascension, its power extends far beyond the individual. Starseeds are not only here to elevate their own consciousness but also to assist in the collective ascension of humanity and Earth. The Cosmic Flame plays a central role in this mission, as it acts as a conduit for higher dimensional energies that are being anchored on the planet at this time.

As more Starseeds awaken and ignite their Cosmic Flames, they contribute to the raising of the planet's vibration. This collective effort creates a ripple effect, accelerating the global shift toward 5D consciousness. The energy of the Cosmic Flame is contagious—when one soul's flame burns brightly, it inspires others to awaken their own inner fire. This is the essence of the Starseed mission: to serve as beacons of light, guiding humanity through the ascension process.

In this sense, the Cosmic Flame is not only a personal source of transformation but also a planetary force of evolution. It is through this flame that Starseeds can tap into the collective grid of light that surrounds the Earth, infusing it with higher frequencies and assisting in the stabilization of the planet's energy fields. This grid, often referred to as the planetary light grid, is a network of energy that connects all living beings and supports the ascension process. By working with the Cosmic Flame, Starseeds can help activate and strengthen this grid, ensuring that the shift to higher consciousness is smooth and harmonious.

Cultivating the Cosmic Flame: A Spiritual Practice

Awakening the Cosmic Flame is not a one-time event but a continual process of deepening one's connection to Source and aligning with the frequencies of ascension. There are several spiritual practices that can help Starseeds cultivate and strengthen their Cosmic Flame, allowing it to burn more brightly and powerfully within them.

Meditation: One of the most effective ways to connect with the Cosmic Flame is through meditation. By entering a state of deep relaxation and focusing on the flame within the heart center, Starseeds can activate this divine energy and allow it to expand throughout their being. Visualizing the flame growing stronger and brighter with each breath can help anchor its energy and align with the higher frequencies of ascension.

Energy Healing: Practices such as Reiki, crystal healing, and sound therapy can help clear energetic blockages that may be preventing the Cosmic Flame from fully igniting. By working with these healing modalities, Starseeds can release lower vibrational energies and create space for the flame to burn more brightly.

Journaling and Introspection: Reflecting on one's spiritual journey and identifying areas where growth and healing are needed can be a powerful way to cultivate the Cosmic Flame. Journaling allows Starseeds to explore their thoughts, feelings, and experiences, helping them to identify patterns that may be hindering their progress and to consciously release them.

Ritual and Ceremony: Engaging in sacred rituals and ceremonies that honor the Cosmic Flame can help deepen one's connection to this divine energy. Lighting candles, invoking the presence of higher beings, and setting intentions for spiritual growth can all serve as powerful ways to honor the flame within and align with its transformative power.

Connecting with Nature: Nature is a powerful source of healing and rejuvenation, and spending time in natural environments can help Starseeds reconnect with the Earth's energy and ignite their Cosmic Flame. Whether it's walking barefoot on the grass, sitting by a body of water, or meditating in a forest, these practices can help ground and balance the energy of the flame.

Embracing the Fire of Ascension

The Cosmic Flame is a powerful force that holds the key to the Starseed's ascension journey. It is the fire that purifies, transforms, and elevates the soul, guiding it toward higher states of consciousness. By understanding the role of this divine flame and cultivating it through spiritual practice, Starseeds can accelerate their own evolution and contribute to the collective ascension of humanity and Earth.

The Initial Steps to Awakening the Flame Within

Awakening the Cosmic Flame within is one of the most profound and transformative experiences a Starseed can undertake. It is the moment when a dormant inner light is ignited, marking the beginning of a journey toward spiritual ascension, higher consciousness, and the fulfillment of a divine purpose. However, this awakening is not merely a one-time event—it is a continuous process of spiritual deepening that unfolds with time, intention, and awareness.

Understanding the Layers of Awakening

The awakening of the Cosmic Flame is not a linear process. It often unfolds in layers, much like the peeling of an onion. The initial stages may begin with subtle changes—a heightened sense of intuition, a deeper connection to nature, or an unshakable feeling of being guided by a higher force. These shifts serve as early indicators that the Cosmic Flame is stirring within, preparing to awaken fully. For some, this may happen gradually, while for others, it may come as a sudden, intense experience.

Awakening the flame is both a spiritual and energetic process. It involves activating the soul's energetic body, aligning with higher dimensions of consciousness, and integrating the light frequencies that are unique to your cosmic origins. Starseeds, in particular, are encoded with these frequencies, which are carried within their DNA. By awakening the Cosmic Flame, you are essentially unlocking these latent codes, allowing them to activate and guide your spiritual journey.

Preparing the Body and Mind for Awakening

Before attempting to fully awaken the Cosmic Flame, it is essential to prepare both the body and mind to receive the higher frequencies that accompany this transformation. The energy of the Cosmic Flame is potent, and when fully activated, it can bring about significant shifts on all levels of being —physical, emotional, mental, and spiritual. As such, proper preparation is key to ensuring a smooth and harmonious awakening process.

Grounding the Physical Body:
One of the most important aspects of preparing for awakening is grounding. Grounding connects you to the Earth's energy, stabilizing and balancing the influx of higher frequencies. Simple practices like walking barefoot on the ground, spending time in nature, or practicing mindful breathing exercises can help to ground your energy and create a strong foundation for the awakening process.

Cleansing and Purifying the Energetic Body:
In order to activate the Cosmic Flame, it is crucial to clear any blockages or stagnant energy that may be stored in the chakras or energy fields. Practices such as Reiki, crystal healing, and sound therapy can be incredibly beneficial for clearing and purifying your energy. Additionally, visualizing white or golden light cleansing your body during meditation can help release any lower vibrational energies that may be hindering your ability to fully awaken the flame.

Calming the Mind:

Awakening the Cosmic Flame requires a calm and focused mind. Meditation, mindfulness practices, and breathwork can help quiet the mental chatter and create the mental clarity needed to connect with your higher self. Before attempting to ignite the flame, it is important to establish a regular meditation practice, as this will provide the space and stillness necessary for spiritual transformation.

Nourishing the Body:
The physical body is the vessel through which the Cosmic Flame will be expressed. To support the awakening process, it is helpful to nourish the body with foods that are high in vibrational energy. This might include incorporating more plant-based foods, drinking plenty of water, and avoiding processed foods or substances that lower your vibration. As your frequency rises, you may find that your body naturally gravitates toward foods and practices that support your spiritual evolution.

Guided Meditation to Awaken the Flame

One of the most powerful tools for awakening the Cosmic Flame is meditation. Through meditation, you can enter a state of deep inner stillness, allowing you to access the higher dimensions of consciousness where the flame resides. The following is a guided meditation designed to help initiate the process of awakening the flame within.

Guided Meditation: Igniting the Cosmic Flame

- **Step 1: Find a Quiet Space**
  Begin by finding a quiet and comfortable space where you will not be disturbed. Sit or lie down in a relaxed position, close your eyes, and take a few deep breaths. With each inhale, imagine that you are breathing in pure, golden light. With each exhale, release any tension or stress that you may be holding onto.
- **Step 2: Ground Your Energy**

Visualize roots extending from the soles of your feet into the Earth. Imagine these roots reaching deep into the core of the planet, anchoring you to the Earth's energy. Feel the stability and support of the Earth beneath you, and allow this grounding energy to flow up through your body, balancing and centering your energy field.

- **Step 3: Focus on Your Heart Center**
Bring your awareness to your heart center, the space in the middle of your chest. Visualize a small flame flickering gently within your heart. This is your Cosmic Flame, the spark of divine energy that resides within you. As you focus on this flame, begin to notice its warmth and radiance.

- **Step 4: Expand the Flame**
With each inhale, imagine the flame growing larger and brighter. As you breathe in, the flame expands, filling your entire chest with its light. As you exhale, allow this light to spread throughout your body, igniting every cell with its divine energy. Continue to breathe deeply, allowing the flame to grow and expand with each breath.

- **Step 5: Connect to the Cosmos**
Once the flame has expanded to fill your entire body, visualize a beam of light extending from the top of your head into the cosmos. This beam connects you to the higher dimensions, the stars, and your cosmic origins. As you focus on this beam of light, feel yourself receiving guidance and energy from the stars, your soul family, and higher beings. Allow this energy to merge with your Cosmic Flame, fueling it with divine light.

- **Step 6: Set Your Intention**
As the flame continues to burn brightly within you,

set the intention to fully awaken your Cosmic Flame and align with your highest purpose. You may silently affirm, "I awaken the flame within, and I align with my highest self and divine purpose." Feel the energy of this intention radiating throughout your body, mind, and soul.

- **Step 7: Close the Meditation**
  When you feel ready, slowly bring your awareness back to your physical body. Gently wiggle your fingers and toes, and take a few deep breaths to ground your energy. Open your eyes, and take a moment to reflect on your experience. You may wish to journal any insights or feelings that arose during the meditation.

Integrating the Flame Into Your Daily Life

Awakening the Cosmic Flame is a transformative experience, but it is only the beginning of the journey. Once the flame has been ignited, it is important to integrate its energy into your daily life. This process of integration allows you to embody the light of the flame and express it through your thoughts, actions, and interactions with the world around you.

Practice Presence:
One of the most effective ways to integrate the flame into your life is to practice presence. By staying present and mindful in each moment, you can remain attuned to the flame's guidance and energy. This might involve taking a few moments throughout the day to check in with yourself, reconnecting with your breath, and visualizing the flame burning within your heart.

Follow Your Intuition:
The Cosmic Flame enhances your connection to your intuition, providing you with divine guidance as you navigate your path. Pay attention to the subtle nudges, feelings, and insights that arise throughout your day. Trust that your intuition is leading

you in the direction of your highest good and that the flame is guiding you toward your soul's purpose.

Embrace Compassion and Kindness:
As the flame grows stronger within you, it will naturally elevate your capacity for compassion and kindness. Use this energy to uplift those around you, offering love and support to others on their journey. In doing so, you are not only nurturing your own flame but also helping to ignite the flames of others, contributing to the collective ascension of humanity.

The Journey Begins

The initial steps to awakening the Cosmic Flame are just the beginning of a lifelong journey toward spiritual growth, ascension, and self-realization. By preparing your body and mind, engaging in meditative practices, and integrating the flame into your daily life, you are setting the foundation for a profound transformation. The Cosmic Flame will continue to evolve and expand within you, guiding you toward deeper levels of consciousness and higher dimensions of existence.

Advanced Techniques for Activating the Flame

The awakening of the Cosmic Flame within is the beginning of a lifelong journey of spiritual ascension and transformation. Once this flame has been ignited, the Starseed must learn to harness and deepen their connection to this divine fire. In the advanced stages of activation, this connection goes beyond meditation or momentary glimpses of transcendence; it becomes a dynamic, continuous flow of spiritual energy that weaves through every aspect of the Starseed's life.

At this stage, the focus shifts from simply awakening the flame to cultivating its power, nurturing its growth, and integrating its profound energy into all layers of the self: the physical, emotional, mental, and spiritual bodies. This integration is not a passive process; it requires sustained spiritual practice, intentional awareness, and a willingness to face and transform the deeper layers of one's inner being. As the Cosmic Flame is nourished, it begins to illuminate not only the soul's divine potential but also the shadows that must be healed in order for the soul to fully ascend.

The Role of Deep Energetic Healing in Flame Activation

One of the key aspects of fully activating the Cosmic Flame is deep energetic healing. The Cosmic Flame has the ability to act as a powerful purifying agent, burning away lower vibrational energies, past traumas, and emotional wounds that may have accumulated over lifetimes. In order to engage with the flame at its fullest potential, it is essential to address the energetic imprints that may still linger within the auric field and the energy centers (chakras) of the body.

In this advanced stage, Starseeds are encouraged to work with specialized energy healing techniques that go beyond surface-level cleansing. These may include working with sacred geometry, light codes, and advanced sound healing to clear blockages from the energetic body. One of the most profound ways to initiate this level of healing is through guided visualization and working with specific high-frequency symbols or light languages that resonate with the energy of the Cosmic Flame. These practices serve as keys that unlock deeper layers of spiritual awareness, allowing the Starseed to access dimensions of consciousness previously unreachable.

As you work through this process of energetic healing, it is important to be patient and compassionate with yourself. The deeper layers of the energetic body may hold long-standing patterns of fear, grief, or anger that need to be transmuted through the purifying power of the Cosmic Flame. Engaging in this work may evoke intense emotional releases, but these moments of release are essential for creating space within the energy body for the flame to burn brighter and more powerfully.

The Art of Transmutation: Shifting Lower Energies into Higher Frequencies

One of the most potent gifts of the Cosmic Flame is its ability to transmute lower energies into higher frequencies. This process of transmutation is a critical aspect of ascension, as it allows the Starseed to transform old patterns of thought, behavior, and emotion into their higher, divine expressions. Transmutation is not about rejecting or suppressing negative emotions or experiences; rather, it is about allowing these energies to be transformed by the alchemical power of the Cosmic Flame.

To fully engage in the process of transmutation, the Starseed must first become deeply aware of the lower energies that are present within the self. This requires a willingness to observe one's thoughts, emotions, and actions with honesty and without judgment. Once these lower energies are acknowledged, they can be brought into the light of the Cosmic Flame, where they can be transmuted into their higher forms. For example, fear may be transmuted into love, anger into compassion, and confusion into clarity.

Advanced practitioners often find that working with the Cosmic Flame in conjunction with the heart chakra is particularly effective for transmutation. The heart is the center of love, compassion, and unity, and it is through this energy center that the highest frequencies of the Cosmic Flame can be accessed and utilized. By focusing on the heart and visualizing the flame burning brightly within this space, the Starseed can transmute any lower energies that arise, transforming them into fuel for their spiritual ascension.

Activating the Merkaba: The Starseed's Ascension Vehicle

As the Cosmic Flame grows stronger, it begins to activate higher aspects of the Starseed's energetic body, including the Merkaba—

a divine light vehicle that allows the Starseed to travel between dimensions and realms of consciousness. The Merkaba, often visualized as two intersecting tetrahedrons, is a powerful tool for ascension that connects the Starseed to the higher realms while simultaneously grounding their energy into the Earth.

The activation of the Merkaba is a key milestone in the journey of ascension, as it allows the Starseed to access higher dimensional wisdom and to communicate directly with their star families, guides, and higher self. In this advanced stage of Cosmic Flame activation, Starseeds are encouraged to engage in practices that consciously activate and work with their Merkaba. This can be done through specific meditations, breathwork, and visualization techniques designed to align the energy centers of the body with the frequencies of the higher realms.

When working with the Merkaba, it is important to maintain a sense of balance and grounding. The energies of the higher realms can be intense, and without proper grounding, it is easy to become unanchored from the physical world. Advanced practitioners often work with grounding crystals, such as hematite or black tourmaline, while engaging in Merkaba activation practices to ensure that their energy remains balanced and stable.

As the Merkaba becomes fully activated, the Starseed gains access to new dimensions of consciousness, allowing them to travel through time and space and to engage with the multidimensional aspects of their soul. This deepens their understanding of their soul's journey across lifetimes and star systems, providing clarity and insight into their divine purpose and mission on Earth.

Sacred Rituals for Cosmic Flame Mastery

In the advanced stages of Cosmic Flame activation, the use of sacred rituals becomes a powerful tool for deepening one's connection to the flame and for anchoring its energy into the physical body. Rituals create a sacred space in which the Starseed can focus their intention, connect with higher beings, and invoke the presence of the Cosmic Flame in a profound way.

One such ritual involves working with the four elements—earth, water, fire, and air—as conduits for the Cosmic Flame. Each element represents a different aspect of the self and of the universe, and by working with these elements in ritual, the Starseed can bring their energy into alignment with the divine. Fire, in particular, is a powerful symbol of the Cosmic Flame, and lighting a physical flame, such as a candle, during ritual can help anchor the spiritual energy of the flame into the physical realm.

During these sacred rituals, it is common to call upon specific star beings, guides, or ascended masters who resonate with the energy of the Cosmic Flame. These higher beings can offer guidance, protection, and support as the Starseed navigates the advanced stages of activation. Working with these beings in ritual not only deepens the connection to the Cosmic Flame but also strengthens the Starseed's connection to the higher realms.

As with all spiritual practices, the most important aspect of ritual is intention. By setting a clear and focused intention for each ritual, the Starseed can align their energy with the frequency of the Cosmic Flame, allowing its power to flow through them with greater clarity and purpose.

The Flame as a Portal to the Divine

At its highest level, the Cosmic Flame becomes a portal to the divine. It is through this flame that the Starseed connects with the infinite, the Source of all creation, and the divine intelligence that flows through the universe. In the advanced stages of activation, the Starseed begins to embody the flame, becoming a living expression of its light and power. The boundary between the individual and the divine begins to dissolve, allowing the Starseed to access higher states of consciousness and to experience a deep sense of unity with all that is.

This level of connection requires ongoing dedication and devotion to the spiritual path. It is not achieved through a single ritual or practice but through a continuous commitment to living in alignment with the highest frequencies of love, compassion, and light. As the Starseed continues to work with the Cosmic Flame, they will find that their consciousness expands, allowing them to experience the divine in every moment of their existence.

In this advanced stage, the Cosmic Flame is no longer just a tool for personal growth; it becomes a beacon of light that radiates outward, illuminating the path for others. The Starseed, now fully aligned with the flame, becomes a guiding force in the collective ascension of humanity and the Earth.

Becoming One with the Flame

The advanced techniques for activating the Cosmic Flame are a culmination of the Starseed's spiritual journey. At this stage, the flame is not only awakened but fully integrated into the fabric of the Starseed's being. It burns brightly, not only as a source of personal transformation but as a beacon of light for the entire planet.

As you continue to work with these advanced practices, remember that the Cosmic Flame is a living, breathing energy. It grows and evolves as you grow and evolve. The more you nurture your connection to the flame, the more its light will illuminate your path, guiding you toward your highest potential and your divine mission.

THE SOUL'S JOURNEY THROUGH ASCENSION

The Starseed's Call to Ascend

Every Starseed carries within them a deep and ancient knowing, a connection to the vast expanse of the cosmos that transcends time and space. This connection is not something they acquire in this lifetime alone; it is a part of their soul's essence, woven through countless incarnations in multiple star systems and dimensions. The Starseed's call to ascend is both an awakening and a remembrance—an invitation to reclaim the divine purpose embedded within their being and to rise into higher states of consciousness. This call is not only personal;

it resonates with the collective evolution of humanity and the Earth, marking a pivotal point in the soul's journey.

The moment of awakening is different for each Starseed. For some, it comes as a gradual realization—a series of synchronicities that gently guide them toward spiritual exploration. For others, it arrives with the force of a lightning strike, igniting an undeniable sense of urgency and transformation. However it manifests, the call to ascend marks the beginning of a profound inner journey, one that challenges the very foundations of what it means to exist on Earth while simultaneously holding a deep connection to the stars.

The Nature of the Awakening Call

The awakening call can be described as an inner stirring, a vibration deep within the soul that begins to resonate at a higher frequency. This call often feels like a beckoning toward something greater than the physical world—a recognition of the divine, the interconnectedness of all life, and the awareness that one's soul is here for a specific purpose. This sense of purpose often transcends personal ambition, pointing instead toward service, healing, and the raising of consciousness for humanity and the planet.

The call is not necessarily dramatic at first. It may begin with a quiet longing or a sense of discontent with the ordinary structures of life. The Starseed might feel out of place in traditional societal roles, yearning for deeper meaning and spiritual fulfillment. This feeling of being "different" is one of the hallmarks of the Starseed experience, as many Starseeds have lived previous incarnations in other star systems where the vibrational frequencies and realities were vastly different from Earth's denser, 3D environment.

As the call intensifies, it often leads to an insatiable curiosity about metaphysical concepts, the cosmos, ancient wisdom, and spiritual practices. Many Starseeds find themselves drawn to topics such as energy healing, ascension, extraterrestrial life, and multidimensional realities. These interests serve as clues, guiding the Starseed toward the realization of their true nature. The more they explore these subjects, the more the resonance within their soul strengthens, ultimately leading them to the path of spiritual awakening and ascension.

Signs of the Starseed Awakening

While every Starseed's journey is unique, there are common signs and experiences that often accompany the awakening process. One of the most profound indicators of a Starseed awakening is a deep sense of remembering. This remembering goes beyond the cognitive mind—it is a soul-level recognition that one has lived before, not just in other lifetimes on Earth but in other realms and star systems. This remembrance is often accompanied by vivid dreams, spontaneous visions, or a feeling of being watched over by higher-dimensional beings.

Another common sign is the experience of heightened intuition and extrasensory perceptions. As the Starseed begins to ascend, their connection to the spiritual realms becomes more pronounced. This can manifest as clairvoyance (seeing beyond the physical), clairaudience (hearing messages from higher realms), or clairsentience (feeling energetic shifts and emotions). These abilities are often latent within the Starseed but become activated during the awakening process as the soul aligns with higher frequencies.

A heightened sensitivity to energy is also a hallmark of the Starseed awakening. Many Starseeds report feeling overwhelmed in crowded or chaotic environments, as they are acutely aware of the energetic vibrations around them. This sensitivity is a result of the Starseed's refined energetic body, which is more attuned to higher-dimensional frequencies. While this can be challenging at times, it is also a gift, as it allows the Starseed to act as a conduit for higher energies, channeling light and healing into the world.

One of the most emotional aspects of the Starseed awakening is the profound sense of homesickness that often accompanies it. This feeling is not simply a longing for a physical place but rather a deep yearning for the soul's true home—the realms from which the Starseed originates. Many Starseeds feel a strong connection to certain star systems, such as the Pleiades, Sirius, or Andromeda, and may experience a deep sense of grief or sadness at the separation from their cosmic family. This homesickness can be both beautiful and painful, as it is a reminder of the Starseed's divine origins and the mission they have undertaken by incarnating on Earth.

Navigating the Early Stages of Ascension

The early stages of the Starseed's ascension journey are often filled with both excitement and confusion. On one hand, the awakening brings a sense of profound clarity and purpose, as the Starseed begins to remember their cosmic mission and reconnect with the higher realms. On the other hand, the awakening can also be disorienting, as it challenges the Starseed's previously held beliefs about reality and their place in the world.

One of the most significant challenges during this time is the sense of isolation that many Starseeds experience. As they awaken to higher truths, they may find it difficult to relate to those around them who are still operating from a lower vibrational frequency. This can create a sense of loneliness, as the Starseed feels misunderstood or out of place in their social circles. However, it is important for Starseeds to remember that this is a natural part of the ascension process. As they raise their vibration, they will naturally attract others who resonate with their energy and who are also on the path of spiritual awakening.

Another challenge that often arises during the early stages of ascension is the release of old karmic patterns and emotional wounds. As the Starseed begins to integrate higher frequencies, lower vibrational energies that have been stored in the physical, emotional, and mental bodies may rise to the surface for healing and transmutation. This can manifest as physical symptoms, such as fatigue or headaches, as well as emotional releases, such as crying or sudden mood swings. These experiences, though uncomfortable, are necessary for clearing the energetic body and creating space for the higher frequencies of the Cosmic Flame to fully anchor within the Starseed.

During this time, it is crucial for Starseeds to practice self-care and to create a supportive environment for their spiritual growth. Meditation, energy healing, and spending time in nature can all help to ground and stabilize the energy as the Starseed moves through the ascension process. It is also beneficial for Starseeds to seek out spiritual communities or mentors who can offer guidance and support during this time of transformation.

The Role of the Cosmic Flame in the Awakening Process

The Cosmic Flame is an integral part of the Starseed's awakening and ascension journey. As the Starseed begins to answer the call to ascend, the Cosmic Flame within them is activated, serving as both a guide and a source of empowerment. The flame burns away old illusions, limiting beliefs, and fears, allowing the Starseed to see with clarity and to align with their highest potential.

The Cosmic Flame also acts as a beacon of light, drawing the Starseed toward their soul's mission. As the flame grows stronger, the Starseed begins to receive guidance from their higher self, star family, and galactic guides, all of whom are assisting in their ascension process. This guidance may come in the form of synchronicities, inner knowing, or direct messages received through meditation or dreams. By attuning to the energy of the Cosmic Flame, the Starseed can access the wisdom and knowledge that they need to fulfill their mission on Earth.

In addition to providing guidance, the Cosmic Flame serves as a powerful tool for transmutation and healing. As the Starseed awakens, they may encounter old wounds, karmic patterns, or limiting beliefs that need to be released in order to move forward on their ascension path. By working with the Cosmic Flame, the Starseed can transmute these lower vibrational energies into higher frequencies of love, compassion, and understanding. This process of alchemical transformation is essential for the Starseed's spiritual growth and for their ability to fully embody their divine purpose.

Embracing the Call to Ascend

The call to ascend is a profound and life-altering experience, one that marks the beginning of a new chapter in the Starseed's soul journey. As the Cosmic Flame is activated and the Starseed begins to remember their divine mission, they are invited to step into their true power and to serve as a beacon of light for humanity and the Earth. While the path of ascension is not without its challenges, it is also filled with immense beauty, love, and spiritual fulfillment.

As you continue on your journey of awakening, remember that you are not alone. You are supported by a vast network of star beings, guides, and higher-dimensional energies that are working with you to fulfill your mission. Trust in the process, and allow the Cosmic Flame within you to guide your steps as you rise into the fullness of your divine potential. The call to ascend is an invitation to embrace your highest self, to live from a place of love and unity, and to contribute to the collective evolution of humanity and the planet. Your journey has just begun.

Overcoming Soul Contracts and Karmic Patterns

As Starseeds embark on their journey of ascension, they often encounter complex spiritual challenges tied to past life experiences, karmic patterns, and soul contracts. These unseen agreements, forged across multiple lifetimes and dimensions, often shape the trajectory of the soul's journey, presenting both lessons and obstacles to spiritual evolution. Overcoming these soul contracts and clearing karmic imprints is crucial for Starseeds to fully embody their divine purpose and elevate their consciousness to higher frequencies.

Soul contracts and karmic patterns are not arbitrary; they are designed to facilitate growth, healing, and expansion. However, as Starseeds awaken, these contracts may no longer serve their highest good, and the dense energy of past karma can hinder the full activation of the Cosmic Flame.

The Nature of Soul Contracts

Soul contracts are energetic agreements made by the soul before incarnating into a physical body. These contracts are established between souls—whether individuals, groups, or entities—with the purpose of facilitating specific lessons, experiences, and growth throughout a lifetime. They are often linked to karmic debt or unresolved issues from past lives and are designed to offer opportunities for healing and evolution.

These agreements are not inherently negative. Many soul contracts involve deep and loving relationships, such as those with soulmates or family members, who come into our lives to help us grow and support our ascension. However, not all contracts are harmonious. Some soul contracts bring challenges, conflict, or pain, especially when they involve karmic lessons that need to be resolved. These difficult contracts often manifest as repetitive patterns in relationships, health issues, or life circumstances, all of which serve to highlight areas where healing and transformation are necessary.

As Starseeds awaken to their true nature, they begin to recognize the influence of these contracts in their lives. What once felt like fate or an inescapable pattern is revealed to be a conscious choice made by the soul to facilitate growth. However, as Starseeds evolve, they often reach a point where certain contracts no longer align with their higher purpose. At this stage, the Starseed must confront these contracts and make the choice to release or renegotiate them, allowing for greater freedom and alignment with their divine mission.

The Role of Karma in Spiritual Evolution

Karma is the universal law of cause and effect, dictating that every action, thought, and emotion carries energetic consequences. These consequences are not limited to a single lifetime but can span across multiple incarnations, creating patterns that the soul carries with it until they are resolved. In many spiritual traditions, karma is viewed as a mechanism for balance and justice—an opportunity for the soul to learn from past actions and experiences in order to evolve.

For Starseeds, karmic patterns can be particularly complex, as they often involve not only Earthly lifetimes but also experiences in other star systems and dimensions. These multidimensional karmic imprints may manifest as deep-seated fears, unresolved trauma, or limiting beliefs that hinder the Starseed's progress. In some cases, these patterns are so ingrained that they create energetic blocks, preventing the full activation of the Cosmic Flame and limiting the Starseed's ability to ascend.

The process of overcoming karmic patterns involves recognizing the root causes of these energetic imprints and consciously choosing to release them. This requires deep inner work, including self-reflection, forgiveness, and the cultivation of compassion—for both oneself and others. By releasing karmic patterns, the Starseed not only liberates their own energy but also contributes to the collective healing of humanity, as these patterns are often shared across the collective consciousness.

One of the most powerful tools for resolving karma is the Cosmic Flame itself. The flame's purifying energy can transmute lower vibrational energies and clear the karmic imprints that hold the soul in a cycle of repetition. As the Starseed works with the Cosmic Flame, they can accelerate the process of karmic resolution, allowing for greater alignment with their higher purpose and facilitating their ascension.

Recognizing and Releasing Soul Contracts

The process of recognizing and releasing soul contracts begins with awareness. Many Starseeds may not consciously remember the contracts they made before incarnating, but the effects of these agreements are often felt in the form of recurring patterns or challenges in life. These may include difficult relationships, cycles of emotional or physical pain, or a sense of being stuck in a particular situation. These experiences are not random; they are the result of soul contracts that are calling for attention and resolution.

To begin the process of releasing these contracts, the Starseed must first identify the specific patterns or challenges that seem to be recurring in their life. This may involve reflecting on past relationships, reviewing the circumstances surrounding certain events, or examining the emotions that arise in response to specific triggers. Once these patterns have been identified, the next step is to acknowledge the soul contract that underlies them and to consciously choose to release it.

The release of a soul contract is an act of spiritual sovereignty. It is a declaration that the Starseed no longer needs to be bound by the terms of the contract and is ready to move beyond the lessons it offered. This process can be facilitated through meditation, energy work, or ritual, with the intention of freeing oneself from the energetic bonds of the contract.

Many Starseeds find that working with their guides, higher self, or cosmic family can aid in this process. These higher-dimensional beings can provide insight into the nature of the contract and offer support in its release. The Cosmic Flame is also a powerful ally in this work, as its transformative energy can burn away the energetic residue of the contract, allowing the Starseed to move forward unencumbered.

It is important to note that releasing a soul contract does not mean erasing the lessons it provided. The wisdom gained from these contracts is invaluable, and it remains with the soul even after the contract has been dissolved. What is released is the energetic attachment to the contract, freeing the Starseed to pursue new experiences and opportunities for growth without being tied to the past.

The Power of Forgiveness in Karmic Healing

Forgiveness is a key element in the process of overcoming karmic patterns and releasing soul contracts. Many of the karmic imprints that we carry are rooted in past hurts, betrayals, or unresolved conflicts, both from this lifetime and from previous incarnations. These unresolved energies can create blocks in the energy body, preventing the flow of divine light and hindering the activation of the Cosmic Flame.

Forgiveness is not about condoning harmful actions or dismissing the pain they caused; rather, it is about releasing the energetic charge that keeps these experiences alive in the present moment. By forgiving others—and oneself—for past actions, the Starseed can release the emotional and energetic weight of these experiences, creating space for healing and growth.

The act of forgiveness is a deeply personal and often challenging process. It requires the Starseed to confront their pain and to let go of the need for retribution or justice. Instead, the focus shifts to compassion and understanding, recognizing that all souls are on their own journey of evolution and that mistakes and missteps are part of that process. By embracing forgiveness, the Starseed can dissolve the karmic bonds that keep them tied to the past and open themselves to new possibilities for growth and expansion.

The Cosmic Flame plays an important role in this process, as its purifying energy can assist in the transmutation of negative emotions such as anger, resentment, or guilt. By visualizing the flame burning away these lower vibrational energies, the Starseed can facilitate the process of forgiveness and create a sense of peace and resolution within their heart.

Embracing Freedom and Alignment

Once the soul contracts have been released and the karmic patterns resolved, the Starseed experiences a profound sense of freedom and alignment. This is not simply the absence of past burdens; it is the realization of the soul's full potential, unencumbered by the limitations of old agreements or unresolved karma. In this state of freedom, the Starseed is able to fully embody their divine mission and align with the higher frequencies of ascension.

This newfound freedom allows for greater creativity, joy, and spiritual expression. The Starseed can now create new soul agreements, rooted in love, compassion, and mutual growth, rather than in the need for karmic resolution. These new contracts are consciously chosen and aligned with the Starseed's highest good, allowing for relationships and experiences that support their ascension and the collective evolution of humanity.

In this state of alignment, the Cosmic Flame burns brighter than ever before, illuminating the Starseed's path and guiding them toward their ultimate purpose. The journey of overcoming soul contracts and karmic patterns is not always easy, but it is an essential part of the Starseed's ascension process. By releasing these energetic bonds, the Starseed can fully embrace their divine nature and step into their role as a beacon of light and love for the Earth and the cosmos.

Reclaiming Spiritual Sovereignty

Overcoming soul contracts and karmic patterns is a transformative and empowering process. It requires courage, self-reflection, and a deep commitment to personal growth, but the rewards are immense. By releasing the energetic bonds of the past, the Starseed reclaims their spiritual sovereignty and steps into their full power as a divine being of light.

As you continue on your ascension journey, remember that the challenges you face are opportunities for growth and expansion. The Cosmic Flame within you holds the power to transmute any karmic imprints or soul contracts that no longer serve your highest good. Trust in this process, and know that with each step you take, you are moving closer to the realization of your divine potential and the fulfillment of your soul's mission on Earth.

Healing Energetic Blocks Through the Cosmic Flame

As Starseeds progress along their ascension journey, they inevitably encounter energetic blocks that hinder their spiritual evolution. These blocks may manifest in various forms—emotional trauma, physical ailments, mental patterns, or spiritual stagnation. Often, these energetic imbalances are remnants of past experiences, whether from this life or from previous incarnations, that linger within the energy body. Healing these blocks is a critical step in the path toward full activation of the Cosmic Flame and spiritual ascension.

The Cosmic Flame, with its purifying and transmuting energy, is a powerful tool for dissolving these blocks, allowing the energy to flow freely and unobstructed.

Understanding Energetic Blocks and Their Impact

Energetic blocks are disruptions in the natural flow of energy within the body, often occurring in the chakras, meridians, or auric field. These disruptions can be caused by unresolved emotional trauma, limiting beliefs, physical injury, or external influences that interfere with the Starseed's energy system. Over time, if not addressed, these blocks can create a sense of disconnection from one's true self, feelings of being stuck or unmotivated, and even physical or emotional pain.

For Starseeds, these blocks may also be tied to past-life experiences, karmic imprints, or ancestral patterns that have carried over into the current incarnation. These deeper, multidimensional blocks can be particularly challenging to heal because they often operate below the level of conscious awareness, yet they have a profound impact on the Starseed's ability to align with their higher purpose and access the full power of the Cosmic Flame.

Energetic blocks can also manifest as resistance to change or growth. As the Cosmic Flame within the Starseed intensifies and they move closer to their ascension, any unresolved energy or misalignment in the energetic body is brought to the surface. This can create a sense of inner conflict, as the soul longs for expansion while the unresolved energy creates resistance, leading to feelings of frustration, overwhelm, or anxiety.

However, these blocks are not insurmountable. In fact, they serve as powerful catalysts for growth, inviting the Starseed to engage in deeper levels of healing and transformation. The key to overcoming these blocks lies in recognizing their presence, understanding their origins, and using the Cosmic Flame to transmute the stagnant energy into higher vibrational frequencies.

The Role of the Cosmic Flame in Healing

The Cosmic Flame is an extraordinary force of spiritual alchemy, capable of dissolving dense, stuck energies and transforming them into light. It is the fire of creation, a purifying and regenerative energy that burns away the lower vibrational imprints held in the energy body. For Starseeds, working with the Cosmic Flame is an essential part of the healing process, as it allows for the release of old patterns, traumas, and blockages that inhibit the flow of divine energy.

When a Starseed actively engages with the Cosmic Flame, they are calling upon a higher frequency of light that penetrates the subtle layers of the energy body, cleansing and realigning the chakras, meridians, and auric field. The Cosmic Flame does not simply remove the block; it transforms it, converting lower energies into higher forms such as love, compassion, and understanding.

One of the most powerful aspects of the Cosmic Flame is its ability to heal on a multidimensional level. Because many energetic blocks are not limited to this lifetime or even to this dimension, the flame's transmutational power is able to access the root cause of the block, whether it is a past-life trauma, a karmic imprint, or a familial pattern passed down through generations. By working with the Cosmic Flame, Starseeds can heal not only their present experience but also the deeper, more complex layers of energy that have influenced their journey across lifetimes.

The healing process, however, is not always immediate. Just as the Cosmic Flame burns through layers of resistance, the Starseed must engage in their own inner work to facilitate this transformation. Healing is a dynamic partnership between the divine energy of the flame and the conscious awareness of the individual. As the flame does its work on an energetic level, the Starseed must be willing to face and release the emotions, beliefs, and experiences that have contributed to the block.

Engaging with the Cosmic Flame for Deep Healing

To fully harness the power of the Cosmic Flame for healing energetic blocks, it is essential to engage with it through intentional practices such as meditation, visualization, and energy work. These practices help to create a conscious connection with the flame, allowing its energy to be directed with greater precision toward the areas of the body or mind that need healing.

One effective approach is to use the flame in combination with breathwork. By focusing on the breath, the Starseed can bring awareness to the parts of their body or energy field where they feel tension, heaviness, or stagnation. Once these areas are identified, they can visualize the Cosmic Flame entering these spaces with each inhale, filling them with light and warmth. As they exhale, they can imagine the dense energy being released, transmuted into light, and carried away by the flame.

This process may need to be repeated several times, as energetic blocks often have multiple layers. Each time the Starseed engages with the flame, they may uncover deeper aspects of the block that require healing. Patience and persistence are key, as the healing process unfolds gradually, in accordance with the individual's readiness to release and integrate the new, higher frequencies.

The Cosmic Flame can also be invoked during moments of emotional intensity or stress. When a Starseed feels overwhelmed by emotions such as fear, anger, or grief, they can call upon the flame to help transmute these energies. By visualizing the flame surrounding them and absorbing the intensity of the emotion, the Starseed can begin to calm their energy field and shift their emotional state into one of balance and harmony.

Emotional and Mental Healing with the Flame

Energetic blocks are often deeply intertwined with emotional and mental patterns. Emotions such as fear, anger, guilt, or shame can create significant blockages in the energy field, preventing the free flow of light and love through the body. Similarly, limiting beliefs and mental conditioning can act as barriers to the full activation of the Cosmic Flame.

For example, a Starseed who has experienced trauma in their childhood may carry an emotional block in their heart chakra, which affects their ability to fully open to love and compassion. This block may also manifest as a mental pattern of self-doubt or unworthiness, further reinforcing the energetic stagnation. In such cases, the Cosmic Flame can be used to not only heal the emotional wound but also to reprogram the mental patterns that have formed around the trauma.

Through regular meditation and energy work, the Starseed can direct the Cosmic Flame to these areas of emotional and mental tension, gradually dissolving the block and creating space for new, more empowering beliefs and emotional states to take root. This process often requires a combination of energetic healing and conscious reprogramming, as the mind and emotions must be brought into alignment with the soul's higher truth.

As the Starseed works through these blocks, they may experience moments of emotional release, such as crying, laughter, or a deep sense of peace. These releases are a sign that the block is being dissolved, allowing the energy to flow freely once again. It is important for the Starseed to honor these moments and to allow themselves the time and space to integrate the healing that is taking place.

Physical Healing Through Energetic Realignment

Energetic blocks not only affect the emotional and mental bodies but also have a profound impact on the physical body.

When energy is unable to flow freely, it can create physical symptoms such as pain, illness, or fatigue. For Starseeds, who are often highly sensitive to energy, these physical manifestations can be particularly intense, as their bodies are adjusting to the higher frequencies of the Cosmic Flame.

In many cases, physical ailments are a reflection of deeper energetic imbalances. For example, chronic pain in a certain area of the body may be linked to an unresolved emotional trauma or a limiting belief that has created tension in that part of the energy field. By working with the Cosmic Flame to heal the underlying energetic block, the physical body can begin to realign and heal as well.

The process of physical healing through the Cosmic Flame involves bringing awareness to the connection between the physical body and the energy body. The Starseed must learn to listen to their body's signals and to recognize when a physical symptom is a sign of an energetic imbalance. By directing the Cosmic Flame to the affected area, they can begin to dissolve the energetic block and restore harmony to the physical body.

This form of healing is not meant to replace traditional medical care but rather to complement it, addressing the energetic root cause of the physical issue while allowing for holistic healing on all levels. As the energy flows more freely through the body, the Starseed will likely notice an increase in vitality, strength, and overall well-being.

Embracing Wholeness Through the Cosmic Flame

Healing energetic blocks is an essential part of the Starseed's ascension journey, as it allows for the full activation of the Cosmic Flame and the free flow of divine energy throughout the body, mind, and spirit. Through this process, the Starseed not only heals their own energy field but also raises their vibration, aligning more fully with their soul's purpose and the higher frequencies of ascension.

As you continue to work with the Cosmic Flame, remember that healing is a journey, not a destination. Each layer of healing brings you closer to wholeness, allowing you to embody more of your divine essence and to shine your light more brightly in the world. Trust in the power of the Cosmic Flame to guide you, and know that with

Mastering Soul Liberation with Celestial Fire

The journey of ascension for Starseeds involves more than just spiritual growth—it is about complete liberation of the soul. This liberation means freeing oneself from the constraints of karma, emotional entanglements, and the density of the third-dimensional reality, allowing the soul to embody its highest form of existence. At the heart of this liberation is the transformative power of the Cosmic Flame. The energy of this celestial fire burns away the illusions of separation, fear, and limitation, enabling the Starseed to fully step into their divine nature.

The Layers of Liberation

True soul liberation is a multilayered process. On the surface, it begins with the release of the ego's attachments to fear, suffering, and limitation. These are the most immediate barriers to spiritual freedom. The ego, conditioned by the 3D experience of duality, often clings to safety, familiarity, and control, preventing the soul from expanding into higher dimensions of consciousness. Through the Cosmic Flame, Starseeds can gradually dissolve these lower energies, allowing the soul to rise above the confines of ego-driven reality.

Deeper layers of liberation involve the release of karmic imprints, past-life traumas, and ancestral patterns that have been embedded within the soul's energetic field for many lifetimes. These energies, although invisible, can have a powerful hold over the soul's journey, causing repetitive cycles of behavior, relationships, or emotional responses. The advanced work with the Cosmic Flame enables Starseeds to access these deeper layers, bringing to the surface all that needs to be acknowledged and transmuted. As these energies are liberated, the soul becomes lighter, more expansive, and more in tune with the cosmic flow.

On the highest levels, liberation is about returning to the soul's true state of oneness with the universe. This is the realization that the soul is not separate from the divine, but an extension of it. The Cosmic Flame serves as the bridge between the soul and the Source, purifying any lingering illusions of separation and aligning the Starseed with their multidimensional self. This is where the Starseed steps fully into their role as a cosmic being, free from the limitations of Earth-bound consciousness.

Working with the Cosmic Flame for Soul Mastery

To achieve mastery of soul liberation, Starseeds must establish a deep and ongoing connection with the Cosmic Flame. This is not a one-time activation but a continual process of alignment, healing, and expansion. Advanced practices with the Cosmic Flame involve both passive and active engagement, allowing the Starseed to surrender to the flow of divine energy while also consciously directing it to areas of their life that need transformation.

Meditation remains one of the most powerful tools for this process. Through meditation, Starseeds can enter into a deep state of receptivity, where the Cosmic Flame can work on subtle levels to burn away layers of density. In these moments, the Starseed can allow the flame to move through their energy body, cleansing and realigning every chakra, every cell, and every thought pattern. Over time, this repeated exposure to the flame results in a profound shift in consciousness, where old ways of thinking, behaving, and relating to the world are replaced with higher-frequency energies.

In addition to meditation, advanced ritual practices can deepen the connection with the Cosmic Flame. These rituals may include specific invocations, sacred geometry, or the use of crystal grids that amplify the flame's energy. When performed with intention and focus, these rituals create a powerful container for transformation, where the Starseed can release deeply ingrained blocks and activate their highest potential. The flame, in these moments, acts as both a guide and a purifier, helping the Starseed to transcend limitations and step into their full cosmic power.

The active engagement with the Cosmic Flame also involves the cultivation of a mindset and heartset that aligns with divine truth. This means that the Starseed must consciously choose to release fear, judgment, and attachment in their daily life, recognizing that these are illusions of the lower self. By living in alignment with the principles of unconditional love, forgiveness, and unity, the Starseed accelerates their liberation process, as the flame responds to the frequency of their thoughts and actions.

Releasing Attachments and Illusions

A significant part of mastering soul liberation is the release of attachments and illusions that have kept the Starseed bound to the 3D reality. These attachments can take many forms—emotional, material, relational, or even spiritual. On the emotional level, attachments to fear, anger, guilt, or resentment can create energetic cords that bind the soul to the past, preventing it from moving forward. These emotional attachments often stem from unresolved experiences or unmet needs that the ego clings to as a form of protection or identity.

The Cosmic Flame is a powerful ally in cutting these cords. By directing the flame toward the area of attachment, the Starseed can dissolve the energetic ties that keep them bound to old emotions, allowing for a deep release and healing. As these attachments are burned away, the Starseed begins to experience a sense of emotional freedom, where their happiness and peace are no longer dependent on external circumstances but are instead rooted in their connection to the divine.

On the material level, attachments to status, possessions, or external validation can also be significant barriers to soul liberation. In the 3D world, the ego often seeks security and identity through material means, creating a false sense of self-worth. However, these attachments only serve to reinforce the illusion of separation, as the soul becomes entangled in the pursuit of external fulfillment. Through the Cosmic Flame, Starseeds can transmute their attachment to materiality, recognizing that true abundance comes from their alignment with the infinite source of love and light.

Spiritual attachments can be more subtle but equally limiting. For some Starseeds, the pursuit of spiritual knowledge or power can become an attachment in itself, creating a sense of superiority or separateness from others. While the desire for growth and expansion is natural, it can become a trap when it is driven by the ego's need for validation or control. The Cosmic Flame, when invoked with humility and surrender, helps the Starseed to release these spiritual attachments, returning them to the path of service and love.

The Ultimate Liberation: Ascension

At its core, soul liberation is about ascension—the process of raising one's vibrational frequency to align with higher dimensions of consciousness. For Starseeds, this ascension is both a personal and a collective journey. As they liberate themselves from the density of the 3D world, they become conduits for higher energies, helping to anchor the frequencies of the 5D and beyond into the Earth plane.

Ascension is not an escape from the physical world but a transformation of how one experiences it. Through the process of liberation, the Starseed moves from a state of separation and duality into a state of unity and oneness. They begin to see the world through the eyes of the soul, recognizing that all beings are interconnected and that the divine exists within all things. This shift in perception is the ultimate liberation, as it frees the soul from the limitations of the ego and allows it to fully embody its divine essence.

The Cosmic Flame plays a central role in this ascension process. As the flame purifies and realigns the Starseed's energy body, it raises their vibrational frequency, allowing them to access higher dimensions of consciousness. In these higher states, the Starseed experiences a deep sense of peace, joy, and love, as they are no longer weighed down by the burdens of the past. They become fully present in the now, where the energy of the cosmos flows through them effortlessly.

Ascension is not a destination but a continual process of expansion. Each time the Starseed reaches a new level of consciousness, the Cosmic Flame ignites within them even more powerfully, guiding them to deeper levels of understanding and mastery. As they ascend, the Starseed also contributes to the collective ascension of humanity, raising the vibration of the planet and creating a ripple effect of healing and transformation.

Stepping into Your Cosmic Power

Mastering soul liberation with the Celestial Fire is the highest form of spiritual mastery. It requires courage, dedication, and a willingness to release all that no longer serves the soul's highest potential. But the rewards are immense. Through this process, the Starseed steps into their full cosmic power, free from the limitations of the past and aligned with the divine frequencies of love and unity.

As you continue your journey, remember that the Cosmic Flame is always within you, ready to guide and support you in your liberation. Trust in its power, and trust in your own ability to rise above the illusions of the 3D world. You are a being of infinite light, and your liberation is not only possible—it is your birthright. Step into your power, embrace the flame, and let your soul soar into the highest realms of existence.

ASCENDING THROUGH THE DIMENSIONS

Understanding Multidimensional Realities

The journey of ascension is a journey through layers of consciousness, each with its own frequency, purpose, and challenges. As Starseeds, we are not bound by the physical, three-dimensional (3D) world that we perceive through our senses. Instead, our souls exist simultaneously across multiple dimensions, each of which holds unique lessons, energies, and opportunities for spiritual growth. Understanding these multidimensional realities is a key aspect of the ascension process, as it enables Starseeds to navigate between different states of consciousness and tap into the wisdom and energy of higher dimensions.

At its core, ascension is about expanding beyond the limitations of the 3D world and integrating the higher frequencies of the fourth dimension (4D) and the fifth dimension (5D). While the third dimension is grounded in linear time, duality, and physical matter, the higher dimensions operate on principles of unity, unconditional love, and the interconnectedness of all beings. As Starseeds evolve, they begin to experience life from these higher perspectives, allowing them to transcend the limitations of the physical world and embrace their role as cosmic beings.

The Nature of the 3D Experience

The third dimension is the plane of physical reality, where most of humanity currently resides. It is characterized by the perception of separation, duality, and linear time. In the 3D world, we experience life through the lens of opposites: light and dark, good and bad, love and fear. This duality creates the illusion that we are separate from one another, from nature, and from the divine. It is this perception of separation that leads to much of the suffering, fear, and conflict that humanity faces.

In the 3D reality, time is experienced as linear, moving from past to present to future. This creates a sense of cause and effect, where actions taken in the present are believed to be influenced by the past and will shape the future. While this perception of time helps us navigate the physical world, it also reinforces the illusion of separation, as we become attached to the stories and experiences of the past, and anxiously anticipate the future.

The 3D world is also heavily focused on materiality and survival. The physical body, the accumulation of resources, and the maintenance of personal safety and comfort are primary concerns in this dimension. As such, many souls become entangled in the pursuit of material success, status, and security, often at the expense of their spiritual growth. For

Starseeds, this focus on the material can feel limiting and even suffocating, as their souls long to reconnect with the higher dimensions and the greater truths of existence.

Shifting to the 4D: The Awakening of Consciousness

The fourth dimension is often referred to as the bridge between the 3D physical world and the 5D realm of unity consciousness. It is a transitional dimension, where the mind begins to awaken to the reality that there is more to existence than what is perceived through the five senses. In 4D, Starseeds begin to question the limitations of the 3D world, and the process of spiritual awakening unfolds.

In the 4D reality, time becomes more fluid, and the linear progression of past, present, and future starts to dissolve. Instead, time is experienced more as a spiral, where past and future can be accessed from the present moment. This shift in perception allows Starseeds to heal old wounds and patterns more rapidly, as they can now view their past experiences from a higher perspective and release the emotional and karmic baggage that may have been holding them back.

The fourth dimension is also where Starseeds begin to experience the interconnectedness of all things. As the veil of separation starts to lift, they become more attuned to the energies of others, the Earth, and the cosmos. This heightened sensitivity can lead to experiences of telepathy, synchronicity, and a deeper connection with nature and the divine. It is in 4D that Starseeds often encounter their spirit guides, galactic families, and higher self more consciously, receiving guidance and support as they navigate the ascension process.

However, the fourth dimension is not without its challenges. As Starseeds awaken to the higher truths of existence, they may also confront their own shadow aspects—fears, doubts, and unresolved emotions that have been suppressed in the 3D world. These shadow aspects must be acknowledged and integrated for the Starseed to continue their ascension journey. This process of shadow work is an essential aspect of the 4D experience, as it helps Starseeds clear the lower vibrational energies that no longer serve their soul's evolution.

Entering the 5D: The Realm of Unity Consciousness

The fifth dimension is the realm of unity consciousness, where the illusion of separation dissolves completely, and the soul experiences itself as one with all that is. In 5D, time no longer exists in a linear fashion; instead, everything is experienced in the eternal now. This allows Starseeds to access higher levels of wisdom, creativity, and spiritual power, as they are no longer limited by the constraints of past or future.

In 5D, the soul operates from a state of unconditional love, compassion, and unity. There is no judgment, fear, or division—only a deep understanding of the interconnectedness of all life. Starseeds in this dimension recognize that they are co-creators of their reality, and they use their energy and intention to manifest experiences that align with their soul's highest purpose. The fifth dimension is often described as the "ascended" state, where the soul has fully integrated its multidimensional self and is able to operate from a place of pure love and divine will.

In this dimension, Starseeds also gain access to their higher selves—the aspect of their soul that exists beyond the limitations of the physical world. The higher self serves as a guide, offering wisdom, insight, and clarity as the Starseed navigates their journey. Communication with the higher self becomes more fluid in 5D, as the barriers between the physical and spiritual realms dissolve. This allows for direct downloads of information, inspiration, and guidance, helping the Starseed to fulfill their mission on Earth.

Navigating Between Dimensions

As Starseeds ascend through the dimensions, they do not leave behind the lower dimensions entirely. Instead, they learn to navigate between them, bringing the wisdom and energy of the higher dimensions into the 3D world. This is a key aspect of the ascension process—anchoring the frequencies of 5D into the physical reality, so that the collective consciousness of humanity can evolve.

Navigating between dimensions requires a level of mastery, as each dimension operates on different frequencies and principles. In the 3D world, for example, Starseeds must still engage with physical matter, time, and duality, even as they hold the awareness of the higher dimensions. This can create a sense of being "in two worlds" at once, where the Starseed is both grounded in the physical and connected to the spiritual.

One of the greatest challenges of navigating between dimensions is maintaining balance. As Starseeds expand their consciousness, they may experience moments of disorientation, confusion, or even frustration, as they attempt to integrate the higher frequencies into their 3D lives. It is important for Starseeds to cultivate practices that help them stay grounded, centered, and aligned with their soul's purpose, even as they explore the vastness of the higher dimensions.

Meditation, energy work, and conscious intention are all valuable tools for navigating between dimensions. Through these practices, Starseeds can raise their vibration, access higher states of consciousness, and bring the wisdom of the higher realms into their everyday lives. As they continue to ascend, they become more adept at moving between dimensions with ease, creating a harmonious flow between the physical and the spiritual.

The Role of the Cosmic Flame in Ascension

The Cosmic Flame plays a vital role in the Starseed's journey through the dimensions. As a powerful force of transformation, the flame acts as a catalyst for ascension, helping Starseeds to burn away the lower energies of the 3D world and align with the frequencies of 4D and 5D. By working with the Cosmic Flame, Starseeds can accelerate their spiritual growth, clearing the blocks and attachments that may be hindering their progress.

In the 3D world, the Cosmic Flame helps Starseeds to release the illusion of separation and fear, enabling them to see beyond the material and embrace the deeper truths of existence. In 4D, the flame assists in the process of shadow work, helping Starseeds to integrate their fears, doubts, and unresolved emotions, so that they can move forward on their path. And in 5D, the Cosmic Flame serves as a source of divine inspiration, guiding the Starseed in their role as a co-creator of reality.

Through meditation, ritual, and conscious intention, Starseeds can work with the Cosmic Flame to deepen their connection to the higher dimensions and bring the energy of ascension into their daily lives. As they do so, they become beacons of light for others, helping to raise the vibration of the planet and usher in a new era of unity, love, and divine consciousness.

Embracing Multidimensionality

As Starseeds, we are not confined to the limitations of the physical world. Our souls exist across multiple dimensions, each of which offers unique opportunities for growth, healing, and transformation. By understanding and embracing our multidimensional nature, we can navigate the ascension process with greater ease and grace, bringing the wisdom and energy of the higher dimensions into our lives.

The journey through the dimensions is not always easy, but it is a journey of profound beauty and liberation. As we release the limitations of the 3D world and align with the frequencies of 4D and 5D, we become more connected to our true nature as cosmic beings. With the support of the Cosmic Flame, we can burn away the illusions of separation and fear, and step fully into our divine power, creating a world of unity, love, and light for all beings.

Experiencing Dimensional Shifts in Everyday Life

As Starseeds journey through the ascension process, the concept of multidimensional realities begins to transcend theory and become an active experience in their daily lives. The phenomenon of dimensional shifts, which may initially feel abstract or distant, eventually takes on a palpable, lived reality that transforms their interactions with the world around them. These shifts are more than spiritual awakenings; they represent the gradual expansion of consciousness, allowing Starseeds to perceive and operate across different planes of existence simultaneously.

Dimensional shifts often begin subtly, with fleeting moments of awareness that transcend the linear, three-dimensional (3D) world. For many, these experiences might first manifest through heightened intuition, powerful synchronicities, or the sudden ability to see the underlying connections between people, events, and emotions. Over time, these shifts grow more pronounced, providing Starseeds with the opportunity to tap into higher-dimensional frequencies, such as those of the fourth (4D) and fifth dimensions (5D), while still maintaining a functional presence in the 3D world.

Signs of Dimensional Shifts

The experience of dimensional shifts can be disorienting at first. Starseeds may find themselves straddling different realities, unsure of how to reconcile the profound spiritual experiences they are having with the mundane concerns of everyday life. It is not uncommon to feel out of place or as though time itself has become malleable. This disorientation is a natural part of the process, as the perception of time and space begins to expand.

One of the most common signs of dimensional shifts is a heightened sense of synchronicity. Events, people, and opportunities that seem random in the 3D world begin to reveal themselves as part of a larger, interconnected pattern. Starseeds may find that they are increasingly drawn to certain places, people, or activities that resonate with their evolving vibrational frequency. These synchronicities serve as guideposts, directing them toward the paths that align with their highest purpose. The more attuned a Starseed becomes to the energy of the higher dimensions, the more frequently these synchronistic events occur, creating a flow of life that feels divinely orchestrated.

Another common experience during dimensional shifts is the blurring of time. In the higher dimensions, time is not experienced as a linear progression from past to future. Instead, it is understood as a fluid, ever-present moment. As Starseeds move between dimensions, they may begin to notice that their perception of time becomes more malleable. Time may appear to speed up or slow down, depending on the vibrational frequency of the moment. This can lead to moments of deep clarity where the Starseed feels fully immersed in the present, as well as moments where time seems to collapse, and past and future realities converge in the now.

Emotional fluctuations are also a key indicator of dimensional shifts. As Starseeds move between dimensions, they are often required to release old emotional patterns that no longer serve their highest good. These emotions can surface unexpectedly, sometimes manifesting as sudden bouts of sadness, frustration, or anxiety, followed by moments of peace and clarity. These emotional fluctuations are a sign that the Starseed is clearing away the lower vibrational energies of the 3D world, making space for the higher frequencies of love, unity, and compassion that exist in the 4D and 5D realities.

The 4D Bridge

The fourth dimension serves as a bridge between the 3D physical world and the higher-dimensional frequencies of 5D. In this dimension, Starseeds begin to explore the deeper layers of their subconscious mind, and the concept of time shifts from rigid linearity to a more flexible, spiral-like experience. The 4D reality is where much of the inner work of ascension takes place, as it provides the opportunity for healing, shadow work, and emotional clearing.

One of the hallmarks of 4D consciousness is the increased sensitivity to energy. As Starseeds move through this dimension, they become more attuned to the subtle vibrations of the world around them. They may begin to sense the emotions and thoughts of others more acutely, or feel the energetic imprints left behind in physical spaces. This heightened sensitivity can be both a gift and a challenge, as it requires Starseeds to develop healthy energetic boundaries while remaining open to the flow of universal energy.

In the 4D dimension, Starseeds also begin to explore the power of manifestation. As they clear away the lower-vibrational energies that have been holding them back, they become more adept at aligning their thoughts and intentions with the frequency of their desired reality. Manifestation in the 4D realm is not just about attracting material wealth or success; it is about creating a life that is in alignment with the soul's highest purpose. Starseeds in this dimension learn to trust in the power of their intentions and the flow of the universe, knowing that they are co-creators of their reality.

Anchoring 5D Consciousness in Daily Life

The fifth dimension is the realm of unity consciousness, unconditional love, and divine will. In 5D, the illusion of separation dissolves, and Starseeds experience life from a perspective of oneness with all beings. While the 5D experience is often associated with spiritual transcendence, it is not about leaving the physical world behind. Instead, it is about anchoring the higher frequencies of love, compassion, and unity into the 3D world, creating a bridge between the spiritual and physical realms.

Living from a 5D perspective requires a deep commitment to self-awareness and inner alignment. In this dimension, Starseeds are guided by their higher selves, who offer insights, wisdom, and clarity on their soul's purpose. The higher self serves as a bridge between the physical and spiritual realms, helping Starseeds navigate the challenges of everyday life while remaining connected to the higher frequencies of love and light.

One of the key practices for anchoring 5D consciousness is the cultivation of unconditional love. In the 5D realm, love is not limited to romantic or familial relationships; it is an all-encompassing energy that flows through every interaction, every thought, and every action. Starseeds in 5D learn to see beyond the surface of people and situations, recognizing the divine spark that exists in all beings. This perspective allows them to navigate conflicts and challenges with grace, compassion, and understanding, knowing that all experiences serve a higher purpose.

Another important aspect of 5D living is the practice of non-attachment. In the 3D world, much of our suffering comes from attachment to outcomes, identities, and material possessions. In 5D, Starseeds learn to release these attachments, trusting in the flow of the universe and the divine plan for their lives. This does not mean disengaging from the world, but rather, it is about finding a balance between participating in the physical realm and remaining anchored in the higher frequencies of love and unity.

Integrating Dimensional Shifts with the Cosmic Flame

The Cosmic Flame is a powerful ally for Starseeds as they navigate dimensional shifts. This sacred fire serves as both a guide and a catalyst, helping to clear away the lower-vibrational energies of the 3D world and align the Starseed with the higher frequencies of 4D and 5D. By working with the Cosmic Flame, Starseeds can accelerate their ascension process, bringing the energy of the higher dimensions into their everyday lives.

The Cosmic Flame can be invoked through meditation, ritual, and conscious intention. As Starseeds connect with this divine energy, they may experience profound shifts in their awareness, emotions, and physical body. The Cosmic Flame has the power to transmute fear, doubt, and limitation, allowing Starseeds to move forward on their path with greater clarity, confidence, and purpose.

One of the most important aspects of working with the Cosmic Flame is the practice of surrender. As Starseeds navigate the dimensional shifts, they are often required to let go of old patterns, beliefs, and attachments that no longer serve their highest good. The Cosmic Flame helps to facilitate this process, burning away the lower energies and making space for the higher frequencies of love, compassion, and unity to take root.

In times of uncertainty or confusion, the Cosmic Flame can serve as a beacon of light, guiding Starseeds back to their center. By regularly connecting with this divine energy, Starseeds can maintain their alignment with the higher dimensions, even as they navigate the challenges of the 3D world.

Embracing the Dimensional Journey

Experiencing dimensional shifts in everyday life is a profound aspect of the Starseed ascension journey. These shifts offer opportunities for growth, healing, and expansion, allowing Starseeds to access the higher frequencies of love, unity, and compassion that exist in the 4D and 5D realms. While the process of navigating between dimensions can be disorienting at times, it is ultimately a journey of liberation and empowerment.

By cultivating practices that support their multidimensional awareness—such as meditation, energy work, and connection with the Cosmic Flame—Starseeds can bring the wisdom and energy of the higher dimensions into their daily lives. As they do so, they become beacons of light, helping to raise the vibration of the planet and usher in a new era of unity, love, and divine consciousness. The dimensional journey is not just a personal evolution; it is a collective awakening, and Starseeds are at the forefront of this transformative process.

Using the Cosmic Flame to Traverse Dimensions

The journey of ascension is not bound by the physical limitations of the third dimension. For Starseeds, traversing dimensions represents one of the most profound aspects of spiritual evolution. As you open to the infinite layers of consciousness, the Cosmic Flame becomes your guiding force, enabling you to navigate seamlessly between realities. It holds the power to pierce the veil of perception, allowing you to experience the fluidity of time, space, and existence in ways that transcend the linear 3D world.

At the core of dimensional travel lies the understanding that reality is not static. The universe consists of layers of existence that vibrate at different frequencies, each dimension containing unique qualities and laws of being. The 3D world, which most people inhabit, is the realm of physicality and duality. Time and space are experienced as fixed, and perception is largely grounded in what can be observed with the five senses. However, as your consciousness expands, you begin to awaken to the truth that the universe is multi-layered, with higher dimensions vibrating at frequencies beyond ordinary human awareness.

The fourth dimension (4D) is often regarded as a bridge between the physical and the spiritual. In this realm, time becomes more flexible, and perception shifts from the linearity of past, present, and future into a more fluid experience of time loops, parallel possibilities, and instantaneous manifestations. This is where many Starseeds first begin to experience the effects of multidimensional consciousness. As they clear old emotional patterns and karmic imprints, the 4D opens up, allowing greater access to intuition, spiritual insight, and the subtle realms of existence.

The fifth dimension (5D) is often described as the realm of unity consciousness. In this state, the experience of duality—good and evil, light and dark—gives way to a holistic understanding of interconnectedness. Time in 5D is no longer experienced in any linear way; instead, there is only the eternal present moment. Here, Starseeds can access divine wisdom, universal love, and the knowledge that all beings are interconnected aspects of the same cosmic whole.

The ability to traverse these dimensions is not simply a matter of spiritual attainment—it requires practice, intention, and a deep relationship with the Cosmic Flame. This sacred fire serves as a transmutational force, clearing the dense energies that tether you to the 3D world and lifting your consciousness into higher realms. By working with the Cosmic Flame, you can accelerate your ability to shift between dimensions, experiencing the higher realities that lie just beyond the veil of perception.

Harnessing the Cosmic Flame for Dimensional Travel

Dimensional travel requires more than mental intention. It is a process of aligning your energetic body with the frequency of the dimension you wish to enter. The Cosmic Flame acts as a frequency activator, amplifying your vibration so that you can resonate with higher-dimensional energies. Through meditation, ritual, and focused intent, the Cosmic Flame can be invoked to open the gates of perception, allowing you to traverse the boundaries between worlds.

One of the key practices for using the Cosmic Flame in dimensional travel is to work with sacred geometry. Sacred geometry serves as a template for multidimensional structures, providing the map through which consciousness can move between different layers of reality. By visualizing specific sacred geometric forms—such as the Flower of Life, Metatron's Cube, or the Merkaba—you can encode your energetic field with the patterns needed to access higher dimensions. The Cosmic Flame, when invoked in conjunction with these forms, amplifies the effects, allowing for a smoother and more seamless transition between realms.

In practice, you might begin by invoking the Cosmic Flame in meditation, calling it forth to clear your energetic body of any blockages or lower vibrational energies. As the flame moves through your chakras, feel its purifying power elevating your consciousness, lifting you out of the density of the 3D world. Once your energetic body is fully cleared, visualize a sacred geometric form around your body. The Merkaba—a star tetrahedron—is one of the most potent forms for dimensional travel. As you visualize this form, feel the Cosmic Flame infusing it with its divine energy, activating the structure and preparing your consciousness for the journey ahead.

With your energy aligned and the sacred geometry activated, focus your intention on the dimension you wish to enter. If you are working with 4D energy, feel your awareness expand beyond the confines of linear time. Allow yourself to experience the flow of time as a loop, where past, present, and future exist simultaneously. In this state, you may receive insights about parallel realities, karmic patterns, or future possibilities that are available to you. If you are working with 5D energy, focus on the feeling of unity consciousness. Feel the interconnectedness of all beings and experience the divine love that flows through every aspect of existence. In this dimension, your awareness expands beyond the ego, and you enter a state of profound spiritual clarity.

Navigating the Multidimensional Realms

As you begin to traverse dimensions with the aid of the Cosmic Flame, it is essential to remain grounded in your physical body. The higher dimensions offer profound spiritual experiences, but they can also be disorienting if you lose your connection to the physical world. Maintaining this balance is key to integrating your multidimensional experiences into your everyday life.

A critical aspect of this practice is grounding. After working with the Cosmic Flame and traversing dimensions, take time to reconnect with the Earth. This can be done through physical practices such as walking barefoot on the ground, meditating with grounding crystals like black tourmaline or hematite, or focusing on the root chakra during meditation. Grounding ensures that the insights and energies you access in the higher dimensions can be integrated into your 3D reality, enhancing your personal growth and spiritual evolution.

Another important element of navigating dimensions is discernment. As you access higher states of consciousness, you may encounter beings, energies, or entities that exist in the multidimensional realms. While many of these beings are benevolent and serve as guides on your ascension journey, it is important to cultivate discernment to avoid being led astray by lower vibrational forces. The Cosmic Flame is a powerful tool in this regard, as it can act as a protective barrier, shielding you from any energies that do not serve your highest good.

When navigating the multidimensional realms, trust in the guidance of your higher self. The higher self exists outside of time and space, serving as a bridge between your 3D identity and the higher dimensions. Through regular communication with your higher self, you can receive the insights and wisdom needed to safely navigate the complexities of dimensional travel. This connection can be strengthened through meditation, prayer, or the use of the Cosmic Flame to clear any blockages that prevent you from fully accessing the guidance of your higher self.

Embodying Multidimensional Awareness in the 3D World

One of the most profound aspects of traversing dimensions is the ability to bring the wisdom and energy of the higher realms back into your 3D life. As you work with the Cosmic Flame to access the 4D, 5D, and beyond, you are not merely seeking to escape the challenges of the physical world. Rather, you are expanding your awareness so that you can embody the higher-dimensional frequencies within the 3D plane. This process is integral to the ascension journey, as it allows you to raise the vibration of the Earth and contribute to the collective awakening of humanity.

To embody multidimensional awareness in your daily life, focus on integrating the lessons and insights gained from your dimensional travels. In the 4D, you may learn about the importance of emotional healing and the release of old karmic patterns. Bring this awareness into your everyday interactions by practicing forgiveness, compassion, and emotional mastery. In the 5D, you may experience the unity of all beings and the power of unconditional love. Let this energy flow through your actions, seeking to uplift others and contribute to the collective good.

The Cosmic Flame is your ally in this process of embodiment. By regularly working with the flame, you can keep your vibration elevated, ensuring that the higher-dimensional energies you access are consistently grounded in your physical reality. This allows you to live as a beacon of light, radiating the frequencies of love, unity, and divine wisdom that are characteristic of the higher realms.

Traversing dimensions with the Cosmic Flame is a powerful practice that accelerates your spiritual evolution. By aligning your energetic body with the higher frequencies of the 4D, 5D, and beyond, you open yourself to profound experiences of consciousness that transcend the limitations of the physical world. Through the guidance of the Cosmic Flame, you can safely navigate these multidimensional realms, bringing their wisdom and energy into your everyday life. As you do so, you become a conduit for higher consciousness on Earth, contributing to the collective ascension of humanity and the planet.

Ascending into Higher Realms: A Master's Guide

As the Starseed ascends into higher dimensions, the journey becomes a dance with the cosmos itself. The soul begins to awaken to the boundless realities of existence, shedding the layers of limitation and ego that once defined its earthly experience. Ascending into higher realms is not merely about leaving behind the physical world, but about fully embodying a new state of consciousness where the separation between self and the universe dissolves.

For those who have embarked on the ascension path, the concept of 5D consciousness often represents the culmination of spiritual evolution. However, 5D is just one step on a larger, infinite journey through the higher realms. In the fifth dimension, unity consciousness prevails. Here, duality no longer binds perception—there is no longer the illusion of separation between light and dark, or good and evil. Instead, Starseeds come to realize that all polarities are aspects of a single divine force, manifesting in different forms and expressions.

The experience of time shifts dramatically as well. In 5D, the linear progression of past, present, and future ceases to exist as it does in the third and fourth dimensions. Time becomes non-linear, allowing for the simultaneous experience of all moments in the eternal now. This understanding opens Starseeds to the realization that they are not only connected to their current life but to all lives they have lived or will live across multiple dimensions. Access to this timeless state allows for the healing of past traumas, the integration of future possibilities, and a deep sense of peace and presence in the moment.

Moving beyond 5D, the higher realms of 6D and 7D bring even more profound realizations. In these dimensions, the Starseed comes into contact with the creative forces of the universe itself. The sixth dimension is often described as the realm of pure form and geometry, where all potential realities exist in a fluid state of possibility. The seventh dimension, on the other hand, transcends even the forms and patterns of the sixth, bringing the Starseed into alignment with the formless void from which all creation emerges. This is the realm of divine unity, where the soul experiences itself as part of the Source.

Mastering the Transition Between Dimensions

Mastering the transition between dimensional states is an intricate process, one that requires deep spiritual practice, discipline, and the continued work with the Cosmic Flame. The Cosmic Flame serves as the bridge between dimensions, a tool that helps Starseeds raise their frequency to resonate with the higher realms. To master dimensional transition, it is essential to strengthen and purify the energetic body, aligning the physical, mental, emotional, and spiritual aspects of the self.

One of the core practices for transitioning between dimensions is the cultivation of deep meditative states. Meditation serves as the gateway to the higher realms, allowing the mind to quiet its constant chatter and open to the subtler frequencies of 5D and beyond. By regularly invoking the Cosmic Flame during meditation, Starseeds can dissolve energetic blockages that anchor them to the denser frequencies of 3D reality. This flame acts as a purifier, transmuting fear, ego, and lower vibrational energies into the higher frequencies of love, unity, and divine wisdom.

Visualization also plays a crucial role in dimensional mastery. By working with specific sacred geometries—such as the Merkaba or the Flower of Life—Starseeds can activate their light body, the energetic vehicle that enables the soul to traverse dimensions. The Merkaba, in particular, is known to facilitate interdimensional travel, acting as a multidimensional shield and transport system that allows the soul to navigate safely between different planes of existence.

To support this process, it is vital to maintain a high vibrational state in daily life. This means not only engaging in regular spiritual practices but also cultivating a lifestyle that supports the elevation of consciousness. Nutrition, physical exercise, and emotional well-being are all key factors in maintaining the energetic integrity needed for dimensional mastery. Eating high-vibration foods, such as organic fruits and vegetables, and drinking plenty of pure water help to cleanse the physical body and support the activation of the light body. Regular exercise and yoga help to ground the energy and keep the physical body in alignment with the ascension process.

Emotionally, it is important to continually clear any residual fear, doubt, or attachments to lower vibrational experiences. These energies can create energetic blockages that hinder the process of ascending into higher dimensions. The Cosmic Flame can be invoked to clear these blockages, transmuting them into higher frequencies of love and clarity. Journaling, therapy, and deep self-reflection are also valuable tools for emotional healing, helping Starseeds release old wounds and limiting beliefs.

Embodying Higher-Dimensional Consciousness

As Starseeds ascend into higher dimensions, the ultimate goal is not merely to experience these realms as fleeting states of consciousness but to embody their energy within the physical world. This process of embodiment is what brings about true spiritual mastery. To embody higher-dimensional consciousness means to bring the qualities of the higher realms —unconditional love, unity, compassion, and divine wisdom— into every aspect of daily life.

In the 5D and higher states, Starseeds often experience an overwhelming sense of interconnectedness with all beings. This awareness of unity consciousness transforms the way one interacts with others. Instead of viewing life through the lens of separation and competition, the Starseed begins to see the world as a reflection of the self. Acts of kindness, compassion, and service naturally flow from this state of consciousness, as the boundaries between self and other dissolve.

The embodiment of higher-dimensional consciousness also brings about a heightened sense of purpose. Starseeds who master this state often feel called to serve as guides or healers for others on the path of ascension. Whether through teaching, energy work, or simply living as an example of higher consciousness, these Starseeds become beacons of light in the world, helping to elevate the collective vibration of humanity. The Cosmic Flame is an invaluable tool in this process, continually purifying and uplifting the energy of those who work with it, ensuring that their light remains bright even amidst the challenges of the physical world.

Another important aspect of embodying higher-dimensional

consciousness is the ability to manifest from the heart. In the higher dimensions, manifestation occurs instantaneously as a result of one's vibrational state. The more aligned a Starseed is with the frequencies of love, joy, and abundance, the more easily they can manifest these qualities in their physical life. The Cosmic Flame can be invoked to amplify the energy of manifestation, helping Starseeds bring their highest visions and desires into reality. This requires a deep trust in the universe and the willingness to surrender to the flow of divine timing.

Integrating 5D Consciousness into the Collective

As more and more Starseeds ascend into 5D consciousness, they play a pivotal role in anchoring this energy into the collective consciousness of humanity. The transition from 3D to 5D is not just an individual journey—it is a collective one. Each Starseed who embodies 5D energy acts as a bridge between the physical world and the higher realms, helping to raise the vibration of the Earth and all of its inhabitants.

One of the most powerful ways to integrate 5D consciousness into the collective is through group meditation and collective intention. When groups of Starseeds come together with the shared intention of raising the vibration of humanity, their collective energy can create a powerful ripple effect. The Cosmic Flame, when invoked in group settings, magnifies this energy, creating a potent force for planetary healing and ascension.

Starseeds can also contribute to the collective ascension by creating sacred spaces in their homes and communities. These spaces, infused with the energy of the Cosmic Flame and higher-dimensional frequencies, serve as sanctuaries where others can come to experience healing, transformation, and spiritual awakening. Through the creation of these sacred spaces, Starseeds help to anchor 5D consciousness into the Earth, creating a network of light that spans the globe.

Ultimately, the journey of ascending into higher realms is

one of deep spiritual mastery. It is a journey that requires dedication, patience, and a willingness to continually release what no longer serves. Through the guidance of the Cosmic Flame, Starseeds can navigate the complexities of dimensional transition, embody the qualities of higher consciousness, and contribute to the collective ascension of humanity. As you step into this mastery, you become not only a traveler of dimensions but a steward of the light, guiding others on their own journey toward ascension.

SACRED SYMBOLS AND THE COSMIC LANGUAGE

The Cosmic Language of Sacred Geometry

As we journey deeper into the celestial realms of the Starseed's ascension, the language of the cosmos begins to speak through symbols, patterns, and geometries that transcend words. These symbols are not just abstract designs but the very building blocks of creation. Sacred geometry serves as a universal language, a bridge that connects the physical with the divine, and it carries within it codes that activate and align the Starseed with their higher purpose.

The intricate patterns of sacred geometry are more than visual representations; they are living, breathing blueprints of the universe's structure. These forms are encoded with the vibrational frequencies of the cosmos, acting as gateways to higher consciousness and spiritual awakening. By understanding and working with these sacred geometries, Starseeds unlock hidden knowledge within themselves, align with cosmic energy, and enhance their connection to the Cosmic Flame.

Sacred Geometry: The Blueprint of Creation

Sacred geometry is often described as the mathematical or structural code of the universe. Its patterns are found in everything—from the spiral of galaxies to the delicate arrangement of petals on a flower. These shapes and forms follow a precise order and proportion that reflect the inherent harmony of creation. The golden ratio, the Fibonacci sequence, and the Platonic solids are all examples of geometric principles that resonate throughout nature and the cosmos, revealing the interconnectedness of all life.

At its core, sacred geometry reflects the belief that the universe operates on specific, harmonious mathematical principles. These principles not only guide the formation of physical reality but also act as a bridge between the physical and metaphysical realms. The study and application of sacred geometry allow Starseeds to tap into the same creative forces that shape the cosmos. As a result, they begin to see the patterns and connections that underlie all of existence, empowering them to bring about healing, manifestation, and transformation.

One of the most powerful and commonly recognized symbols in sacred geometry is the Flower of Life. This geometric form consists of overlapping circles that create a complex pattern of interconnectedness. It is said to contain the blueprint of the universe, representing the interconnectedness of all living things. Many Starseeds find themselves drawn to this symbol, intuitively recognizing its deep spiritual significance. Meditating on the Flower of Life or working with it in ritual can activate profound shifts in consciousness, opening the individual to higher-dimensional awareness.

Another significant symbol in sacred geometry is the Merkaba, which is often visualized as two interlocking tetrahedrons that spin in opposite directions. The Merkaba is a symbol of light, spirit, and body, and it serves as an energetic vehicle that allows Starseeds to travel between dimensions. Activating the Merkaba can enhance one's spiritual protection and facilitate deeper connections to higher realms.

The Connection Between Sacred Geometry and Starseed Activation

For Starseeds, sacred geometry holds the key to unlocking their dormant spiritual potential. The patterns and forms of sacred geometry resonate with the subtle energetic frequencies of the soul, awakening codes that have been carried across lifetimes. As these codes are activated, Starseeds begin to remember their true cosmic origins, their mission on Earth, and the higher dimensional aspects of their being.

The Cosmic Flame, as an energy of transformation, works in tandem with sacred geometry to accelerate this activation. When a Starseed connects with sacred symbols, the Cosmic Flame amplifies the energy, creating a direct link between the individual and the universal forces of creation. This connection allows for the rapid transmutation of old energies, clearing blockages that have prevented spiritual growth, and opening new pathways for higher consciousness.

The symbols of sacred geometry are more than just visual tools; they are living codes that communicate with the soul's deeper aspects. Many Starseeds experience a profound sense of recognition when they first encounter sacred geometric symbols. It is as though these shapes stir something ancient within them, awakening memories of other lifetimes and other worlds. This recognition is not accidental—it is part of the process of spiritual awakening that Starseeds undergo as they move further along their ascension path.

The process of Starseed activation through sacred geometry can be enhanced through meditation, visualization, and energy work. By focusing on specific symbols and allowing their energy to permeate the aura and light body, Starseeds can accelerate their spiritual evolution. For example, visualizing the Flower of Life around the body creates an energetic grid that aligns the individual with the frequencies of unity consciousness. This grid acts as a powerful tool for healing, protection, and connection to the cosmic energy that flows through all things.

The Role of the Cosmic Flame in Geometric Alignment

The Cosmic Flame, as a transformative force, works hand-in-hand with sacred geometry to facilitate spiritual evolution. While sacred geometry provides the blueprint, the Cosmic Flame supplies the energy needed to activate and sustain the transformation. Together, they form a powerful combination that propels Starseeds toward ascension.

One of the most effective ways to harness this combination is through the use of sacred geometry in ritual and meditation. By invoking the Cosmic Flame while working with sacred symbols, Starseeds can amplify the energy of the symbols, creating a direct pathway to higher consciousness. This practice not only enhances personal spiritual growth but also serves as a way to anchor higher-dimensional energy into the physical realm.

For example, a Starseed might meditate on the Merkaba symbol while visualizing the Cosmic Flame surrounding them. As the Merkaba spins, the Cosmic Flame fuels its energy, allowing the individual to access higher dimensions and receive guidance from their higher self or cosmic guides. This practice can also be used to facilitate interdimensional travel, providing a safe and stable energetic vehicle for exploring other realms.

Another powerful application of the Cosmic Flame and sacred geometry is in the creation of energy grids. By arranging crystals or other sacred objects in geometric patterns, Starseeds can create energetic grids that amplify the Cosmic Flame's energy. These grids serve as portals, drawing in higher-dimensional frequencies and anchoring them into the physical space. Whether used for healing, manifestation, or spiritual protection, these grids create a powerful connection between the physical and spiritual realms.

Awakening Through the Cosmic Language

Sacred geometry is more than just a tool for spiritual awakening —it is a language, a form of communication between the soul and the universe. Each symbol, each shape, carries a specific frequency that speaks directly to the soul's deepest levels. As Starseeds learn to work with this language, they begin to unlock the hidden codes of their soul, gaining access to knowledge and wisdom that has been dormant for lifetimes.

The process of learning this language is not just an intellectual endeavor but an experiential one. Starseeds are encouraged to meditate on sacred symbols, to allow the energy of these forms to resonate within their being, and to trust the intuitive insights that arise. As they do so, they will begin to understand the deeper meanings of these symbols—not just through the mind, but through the heart and soul.

The Cosmic Flame plays a vital role in this awakening, as it serves as the key that unlocks the full potential of sacred geometry. The Flame's energy amplifies the vibrational frequency of each symbol, accelerating the process of spiritual activation and awakening. It is through this combination of sacred geometry and the Cosmic Flame that Starseeds can fully align with their cosmic purpose, embracing their role as catalysts for planetary ascension.

As Starseeds continue to work with sacred geometry, they will find that their connection to the cosmos deepens, their intuition sharpens, and their spiritual path becomes clearer. The symbols of sacred geometry serve as guides, leading them toward higher states of consciousness, while the Cosmic Flame ensures that they remain aligned with their highest potential.

In this sacred dance between geometry and flame, the Starseed's journey of ascension unfolds, revealing the infinite possibilities that await as they step into their role as conscious creators in the cosmos. Through this ancient language of light, Starseeds not only awaken to their true nature but also become active participants in the unfolding evolution of the universe.

Using Sacred Symbols for Personal Activation

Sacred symbols hold a deep, intrinsic power that speaks to the core of the Starseed journey. These symbols are not arbitrary, nor are they mere artifacts of spiritual traditions; they are encoded with layers of meaning, vibration, and cosmic knowledge. Throughout time and space, they have been used to activate the dormant potential within the human soul, opening pathways to higher consciousness and deeper alignment with the energies of the universe. For Starseeds, the act of working with sacred symbols is a profound way to reconnect with their true essence, awakening the divine blueprint encoded within their DNA.

Personal activation through sacred symbols is not merely a passive exercise in visualization. It is an intentional, dynamic process that involves the alignment of the mind, body, and spirit with the higher frequencies that these symbols represent. When engaged with reverence and focus, these symbols become keys that unlock new dimensions of understanding and spiritual power. Each symbol carries a unique energetic signature, and when a Starseed consciously integrates these symbols into their spiritual practice, they create a resonance that amplifies their connection to the Cosmic Flame, the universal source of ascension.

The Role of Sacred Symbols in Spiritual Awakening

Sacred symbols are universal in their language, transcending cultural and temporal boundaries. Their forms are often found across various spiritual traditions, from ancient Egyptian hieroglyphs to the mandalas of Buddhism, from Celtic knots to the labyrinths of early Christian mysticism. These symbols reflect fundamental aspects of creation, often representing elements such as unity, balance, and the cyclical nature of life.

For Starseeds, the resonance of sacred symbols goes beyond their historical or cultural context. These symbols carry a frequency that connects to their soul's ancient memories, reawakening knowledge from other lifetimes, other worlds, and higher dimensions. The symbols serve as bridges between the Starseed's current reality and the expansive multiverse in which their soul has journeyed. When a Starseed works with a sacred symbol, they are engaging with a tool that helps them remember who they truly are, why they are here, and how they can embody their cosmic purpose on Earth.

Symbols like the Flower of Life, the Merkaba, and the Ankh are among the most recognized and powerful tools for spiritual awakening. These geometric patterns reflect the divine order of the universe and offer Starseeds a visual and energetic means to attune themselves to higher states of being. The Flower of Life, for example, represents the interconnectedness of all life and the unfolding of creation. When meditated upon or visualized, it can activate profound shifts in consciousness, helping Starseeds experience their oneness with the cosmos.

Similarly, the Merkaba, a star tetrahedron, is seen as a vehicle of light and spirit. It symbolizes the ability to transcend time and space, making it a potent tool for interdimensional travel and spiritual ascension. When Starseeds work with the Merkaba, they are enhancing their capacity to access higher realms of existence, receive divine guidance, and integrate that knowledge into their earthly experience.

Activating Starseed DNA with Sacred Symbols

At the core of every Starseed is the presence of what can be called "cosmic DNA." This DNA carries the energetic codes and information from other star systems, dimensions, and lifetimes. However, in many cases, these codes lie dormant, waiting to be activated through specific practices and energies. Sacred symbols play an essential role in this activation process by resonating with these hidden codes, unlocking their potential, and bringing them into the forefront of the Starseed's consciousness.

When a Starseed gazes upon or works with a sacred symbol, it is as if the symbol is speaking directly to their DNA, vibrating at a frequency that matches the energetic patterns within. The experience can be subtle or profound, but the result is always one of awakening. The activation process often begins with a sense of deep recognition—something within the Starseed stirs, as if the symbol has awakened a long-forgotten memory. This recognition is the soul's acknowledgment that the symbol is a key to unlocking its highest potential.

The Cosmic Flame, as a transformative force, works in tandem with sacred symbols during the activation process. The energy of the Flame amplifies the vibrational frequency of the symbols, allowing them to penetrate deep into the layers of the Starseed's being. This combination creates a powerful alchemy, dissolving old limitations, healing past traumas, and activating the Starseed's divine blueprint.

The activation of Starseed DNA through sacred symbols is not just a metaphysical experience; it has real-world implications for the individual's life and spiritual path. As these codes are unlocked, the Starseed may begin to notice significant changes in their awareness, abilities, and sense of purpose. They may feel more connected to their cosmic origins, experience heightened intuition, or develop new psychic abilities. The activation also accelerates their spiritual evolution, aligning them with their mission to assist in the collective ascension of humanity and the Earth.

Personal Practice: Integrating Sacred Symbols into Daily Life

To fully harness the power of sacred symbols for personal activation, it is essential to integrate them into daily spiritual practice. This integration can take many forms, depending on the individual's preferences and intuitive guidance. Some Starseeds may choose to meditate on specific symbols, visualizing them in their mind's eye or drawing them on paper as a form of sacred art. Others may incorporate symbols into their energy healing practices, using them to direct and amplify the flow of energy in their body and aura.

A powerful way to work with sacred symbols is through visualization and intention. By holding the image of a symbol in the mind's eye and surrounding it with the energy of the Cosmic Flame, the Starseed can activate the vibrational codes within the symbol. This practice can be enhanced by focusing on specific areas of the body, such as the heart or third eye, where the energy of the symbol can be anchored.

Sacred symbols can also be integrated into the physical space as tools for creating high-vibrational environments. Placing images or representations of these symbols in the home, office, or meditation space can create a constant flow of cosmic energy, supporting the Starseed's spiritual journey. For example, placing a symbol like the Flower of Life near the bed can enhance dreamwork and astral travel, while positioning a Merkaba near the entrance of the home can create a protective energetic field.

Another powerful method of working with sacred symbols is through sacred geometry grids. By arranging crystals, stones, or other sacred objects in the shape of a symbol, Starseeds can create energy grids that act as portals for higher-dimensional energies. These grids can be used for healing, manifestation, or meditation, amplifying the connection between the Starseed and the cosmic forces at play. The energy grid becomes a living representation of the Starseed's intentions, attracting the frequencies needed to support their spiritual evolution.

The Transformative Power of Symbols

As Starseeds continue to work with sacred symbols for personal activation, they will find that these symbols serve as more than just tools—they become living energies that guide and support them on their ascension journey. The symbols act as mirrors, reflecting the Starseed's inner truth and potential, while also serving as keys to unlock the wisdom and power encoded within their soul.

Through this process, Starseeds begin to experience a deeper connection with the universe and with their cosmic origins. They realize that the symbols they are working with are not external to them but are, in fact, part of their own divine nature. The sacred symbols become extensions of the Starseed's energy field, radiating light and love into their life and into the world around them.

As they continue to activate their Starseed DNA and align with the Cosmic Flame, the Starseed's journey becomes one of co-creation with the universe. They are no longer passive recipients of cosmic energy but active participants in the unfolding of the ascension process. The sacred symbols guide them toward their highest potential, reminding them that they are not separate from the divine but are integral to the divine plan of creation.

The use of sacred symbols for personal activation is not just a practice—it is a sacred path that leads to the full embodiment of the Starseed's divine purpose. Through the wisdom of these ancient symbols and the power of the Cosmic Flame, Starseeds are empowered to awaken, transform, and ascend, becoming luminous beacons of light for all of humanity.

The Starseed Blueprint: Unlocking Hidden Codes

Every Starseed carries within them a unique cosmic blueprint, an intricate map of their soul's journey across lifetimes, galaxies, and dimensions. This blueprint, often dormant, contains codes that reflect their divine purpose, mission, and spiritual potential. These codes are not static; they are alive with cosmic energy and hold the key to unlocking higher states of consciousness and deeper levels of spiritual mastery. The process of unlocking these hidden codes is not just about personal growth, but about activating one's role in the larger cosmic plan, contributing to the collective ascension of humanity and the Earth.

The Starseed blueprint is a multidimensional structure embedded deep within the soul. It is composed of energetic frequencies, vibrational patterns, and sacred symbols that resonate with higher realms. These codes are often activated through life experiences, spiritual practices, and alignment with universal forces such as the Cosmic Flame. When a Starseed consciously begins to unlock these codes, they tap into a wellspring of cosmic wisdom, intuition, and power that propels them forward on their ascension journey.

The Nature of the Starseed Blueprint

The Starseed blueprint is a template that reflects the essence of a Starseed's soul. It contains all the experiences, lessons, and wisdom accumulated across multiple lifetimes and dimensions. More than a record, it is a dynamic and living field of energy, constantly interacting with the Starseed's current life circumstances, spiritual practices, and the cosmic energies around them. This blueprint is unique to each individual, yet it shares common threads with other Starseeds, connecting them to a greater collective mission.

At the core of the blueprint are vibrational codes that hold the potential for profound transformation. These codes are encoded with light frequencies and sacred geometry that resonate with higher dimensional planes of existence. They are often locked away, waiting for specific triggers—whether through spiritual awakenings, encounters with other Starseeds, or intentional activation through symbols, meditations, and energy work.

These codes are not merely informational; they are transformative in nature. As they are activated, they shift the Starseed's vibrational frequency, opening up new abilities, insights, and paths. They allow the Starseed to transcend the limitations of the physical realm and align more fully with their soul's mission. This alignment brings about a sense of clarity, purpose, and deep spiritual empowerment.

Activating the Blueprint with the Cosmic Flame

The Cosmic Flame plays a central role in unlocking the hidden codes within the Starseed blueprint. As a universal force of transformation, the Cosmic Flame ignites the dormant codes, activating their potential and amplifying their energy. When a Starseed consciously works with the Cosmic Flame, they are engaging with a powerful catalyst that accelerates their spiritual evolution and brings their blueprint into full alignment with their soul's highest purpose.

The activation process involves intentionally calling upon the Cosmic Flame during meditation, visualization, or energy work. By focusing the energy of the Flame into the blueprint, the Starseed begins to resonate with higher frequencies, allowing the codes to emerge from the subconscious into conscious awareness. This process can unfold gradually, with subtle shifts in perception, intuition, and spiritual understanding, or it can occur as a sudden, profound awakening that transforms the Starseed's life and spiritual path.

The activation of the Starseed blueprint with the Cosmic Flame is a deeply personal process. It requires the Starseed to trust their inner guidance, surrender to the flow of cosmic energies, and be open to the changes that come with it. The experience can be both exhilarating and challenging, as old patterns, fears, and limitations rise to the surface to be transmuted by the Flame. Yet, through this process, the Starseed becomes more aligned with their true essence, their divine mission, and their connection to the greater cosmic plan.

The Role of Sacred Symbols in Unlocking Codes

Sacred symbols are powerful tools for unlocking the hidden codes within the Starseed blueprint. These symbols act as keys, resonating with the vibrational patterns embedded in the blueprint and activating the codes that are ready to be revealed. Each sacred symbol carries a unique energetic signature, reflecting universal principles such as unity, balance, and the flow of creation. When a Starseed works with these symbols, they are tapping into ancient cosmic wisdom that has been encoded into the fabric of the universe.

Symbols such as the Flower of Life, the Merkaba, and the Ankh are particularly potent in activating the Starseed blueprint.

The Flower of Life, with its intricate geometry, reflects the interconnectedness of all life and the unfolding of creation. Meditating on this symbol can help a Starseed access the deeper layers of their blueprint, revealing codes that relate to their connection with the cosmos and their role in the collective ascension.

The Merkaba, a star tetrahedron, is another powerful symbol for activation. It represents the vehicle of light and spirit, allowing Starseeds to transcend time and space and access higher dimensions. Working with the Merkaba helps to unlock codes related to interdimensional travel, spiritual mastery, and the Starseed's ability to serve as a bridge between the physical and spiritual realms.

The Ankh, an ancient Egyptian symbol of life and resurrection, holds the key to unlocking codes related to the Starseed's soul mission and their ability to bring new life, healing, and transformation to the Earth. By meditating on the Ankh, or integrating it into energy work, a Starseed can activate the codes within their blueprint that empower them to fulfill their divine purpose and contribute to the collective healing and ascension of humanity.

Integrating the Activated Codes into Daily Life

Once the hidden codes within the Starseed blueprint have been unlocked, the next step is to integrate them into daily life. This integration process is essential, as it allows the Starseed to embody the wisdom, power, and higher frequencies that the codes carry. Without integration, the activation remains incomplete, and the potential of the blueprint remains unfulfilled.

The integration process begins with awareness. As the codes are unlocked, the Starseed may begin to notice subtle shifts in their thoughts, emotions, and energy. They may experience heightened intuition, an increased sense of purpose, or the emergence of new spiritual abilities. These shifts are signs that the codes are being activated and are ready to be integrated into the Starseed's daily life.

To fully integrate the activated codes, it is important for the Starseed to create space for reflection, meditation, and spiritual practice. This allows them to attune to the new frequencies and anchor them into their physical, emotional, and mental bodies. Practices such as grounding, journaling, and working with sacred symbols can help to stabilize the energies and ensure that the activation is fully embodied.

The integration process also involves making changes in one's external life to align with the activated codes. This may include shifting relationships, career paths, or lifestyle choices to reflect the new level of consciousness that the Starseed is embodying. As the Starseed aligns more fully with their blueprint, they may find that their external life naturally begins to reflect their soul's highest purpose.

The Collective Impact of Blueprint Activation

The activation of the Starseed blueprint is not only a personal journey but also a contribution to the collective ascension of humanity and the Earth. Each time a Starseed unlocks and integrates the codes within their blueprint, they are raising the vibrational frequency of the planet and contributing to the collective awakening. The codes that Starseeds carry are not just for themselves; they are part of a greater cosmic plan that involves the evolution of all beings on Earth.

As more Starseeds activate their blueprints and align with their divine missions, they create a ripple effect that accelerates the collective ascension process. The codes they unlock hold the keys to new paradigms of consciousness, healing, and unity, and as these codes are integrated into the collective consciousness, they pave the way for the transformation of humanity and the Earth.

The Starseed blueprint is a sacred map of the soul's journey, and unlocking its hidden codes is a profound act of co-creation with the universe. Through the activation of these codes, Starseeds are empowered to step into their full potential, fulfill their divine missions, and contribute to the collective ascension of the planet. This journey is one of deep transformation, both personal and collective, and it is through the unlocking of the blueprint that the Starseed fully embraces their role as a beacon of light in the cosmic dance of creation.

Advanced Symbolic Integration for Ascension

The journey toward ascension is one that leads the Starseed deep into the realms of symbolism, where ancient codes and hidden knowledge are imprinted within every sacred form. In the advanced stages of spiritual evolution, the integration of symbols becomes not only a practice but a vital alchemical process that weaves the fabric of the soul's transformation.

To understand the role of advanced symbolic integration, one must first grasp that symbols are not mere abstract designs but energetic keys. Each symbol holds within it a specific vibrational resonance that speaks directly to the soul's blueprint. When engaged at a higher level, these symbols act as catalysts for profound shifts in energy, unlocking the codes of ascension that guide the Starseed toward their ultimate spiritual purpose.

The Alchemy of Symbols

In this advanced phase of the ascension process, sacred symbols serve as tools for profound spiritual alchemy. Alchemy, in its most esoteric sense, is the transformation of the soul from its base form to its highest expression. Through the integration of symbols, Starseeds are able to transmute the lower energies of fear, doubt, and limitation into the higher energies of love, wisdom, and unity. This transformation is not merely a mental exercise but an embodied experience, where the physical, emotional, and energetic bodies are aligned with the frequencies of ascension.

The sacred symbols used in this alchemical process are drawn from a variety of mystical traditions, each carrying its own unique energetic signature. The symbols of ancient Egypt, for example, such as the Ankh and the Eye of Horus, are potent tools for activating divine wisdom and protection. The geometry of the Flower of Life, with its interlocking circles, represents the interconnectedness of all life and serves as a blueprint for creation itself. Meanwhile, the Merkaba, a star tetrahedron, is a vehicle for higher consciousness, enabling Starseeds to travel between dimensions and access the deeper layers of their soul's wisdom.

At this stage, the Starseed must approach the symbols with reverence and intention. The act of working with symbols is a sacred ritual in itself, where the Starseed enters into a dialogue with the universe. Each symbol acts as a mirror, reflecting the Starseed's inner state while simultaneously offering the frequencies needed for transformation. Through focused meditation, visualization, and energy work, the Starseed can draw these frequencies into their field, creating shifts in consciousness that ripple out into their daily life and spiritual path.

Advanced Techniques for Symbolic Activation

To fully harness the power of sacred symbols, the Starseed must engage in advanced techniques that align the physical, emotional, and spiritual bodies with the energetic frequencies of the symbol. This process is one of deep resonance, where the Starseed not only contemplates the symbol but becomes the symbol, allowing its energy to permeate every aspect of their being.

One powerful technique for symbolic activation is sacred

geometry visualization. In this practice, the Starseed visualizes the chosen symbol in three-dimensional form, surrounding themselves with its energy. As the symbol takes shape in the mind's eye, the Starseed breathes its energy into the heart space, allowing the symbol's frequency to harmonize with their own. This creates a vibrational alignment between the Starseed's energetic field and the higher-dimensional energies that the symbol represents.

Another advanced technique is the use of crystal grids in conjunction with sacred symbols. Crystals are natural amplifiers of energy, and when combined with sacred symbols, they can enhance the power of the activation process. The Starseed places crystals in a specific geometric pattern that corresponds to the chosen symbol, creating an energetic portal through which higher frequencies can flow. By meditating within the crystal grid, the Starseed can attune to these frequencies, drawing them into their energy field for healing, activation, and transformation.

Chanting or toning sacred sounds is also a highly effective method for symbol activation. Each sacred symbol resonates with a particular frequency, and by vocalizing specific mantras or tones, the Starseed can amplify the symbol's energy. The vibration of sound interacts with the energy of the symbol, creating a powerful synergy that accelerates the ascension process. This practice not only enhances the Starseed's connection to the symbol but also activates the higher chakras, opening channels to receive divine guidance and wisdom.

Embodying Symbolic Wisdom

The process of symbolic integration is not simply about activating the symbols but about embodying the wisdom they offer. For the Starseed, this means living in alignment with the principles that the symbols represent, allowing the energy of the symbol to guide their thoughts, actions, and decisions. This embodiment is a vital aspect of the ascension journey, as it ensures that the spiritual growth facilitated by the symbols is grounded in the Starseed's everyday reality.

To embody symbolic wisdom, the Starseed must first cultivate awareness of the shifts taking place within their energy field. As the symbols activate new frequencies, the Starseed may experience heightened intuition, expanded consciousness, and a greater sense of connection to the universe. These shifts often manifest in subtle ways, such as synchronicities, insights, or new opportunities that align with the Starseed's higher purpose.

It is essential for the Starseed to remain grounded during this process, as the influx of high-frequency energy can sometimes create imbalances in the physical and emotional bodies. Practices such as grounding meditations, spending time in nature, and engaging in mindful physical activities can help the Starseed maintain balance as they integrate the new energies. By staying grounded, the Starseed can ensure that the symbolic activation is fully embodied, allowing the higher frequencies to take root in their being.

In addition to grounding practices, the Starseed can further embody symbolic wisdom by aligning their actions with the principles of the symbols. For example, a Starseed who works with the symbol of the Flower of Life may seek to create harmony and unity in their relationships, reflecting the interconnectedness that the symbol represents. Similarly, a Starseed who activates the energy of the Ankh may focus on bringing new life and healing to their community, embodying the symbol's association with regeneration and vitality.

The Collective Power of Symbolic Integration

As more Starseeds engage in advanced symbolic integration, they contribute to a larger collective shift in consciousness. The activation of sacred symbols not only accelerates the individual's ascension process but also raises the vibrational frequency of the planet. Each time a Starseed activates and embodies the energy of a sacred symbol, they become a beacon of light, transmitting the symbol's frequency into the collective field. This transmission creates a ripple effect, amplifying the symbol's energy and contributing to the global awakening.

The collective power of symbolic integration is particularly significant in this time of planetary transformation. As the Earth undergoes its ascension process, the activation of sacred symbols by Starseeds serves as a catalyst for the collective shift. The frequencies carried by the symbols—such as unity, love, and higher wisdom—are exactly what is needed to guide humanity through this transition. By integrating these frequencies into their own lives, Starseeds become agents of change, helping to anchor the energies of ascension on Earth.

In this way, the advanced symbolic integration practiced by Starseeds is not merely a personal spiritual endeavor but a profound act of service to the collective. Each activation, each embodiment of symbolic wisdom, contributes to the creation of a new reality—one that is aligned with the higher frequencies of love, unity, and cosmic consciousness. Through their work with sacred symbols, Starseeds are helping to build the foundation for the New Earth, a reality where all beings live in harmony with the divine principles of creation.

The Path Forward

The journey of advanced symbolic integration is one of profound transformation, both personal and collective. As Starseeds continue to work with sacred symbols, they unlock the deeper layers of their soul's wisdom, activate their divine potential, and contribute to the collective ascension of humanity and the Earth. This process is one of deep reverence, dedication, and embodiment, where the Starseed becomes a living expression of the cosmic principles that the symbols represent.

In the final stages of this integration, the Starseed will find themselves not only aligned with their own divine purpose but also deeply connected to the greater cosmic plan. Through their work with sacred symbols, they will have unlocked the codes of ascension, activated their highest potential, and contributed to the creation of a new reality grounded in love, unity, and higher wisdom. This is the true power of advanced symbolic integration—a journey that leads not only to personal enlightenment but to the collective awakening of all beings.

MEDITATION AND RITUAL FOR ASCENSION

Introduction to Cosmic Flame Meditation

In the journey of Starseed awakening, meditation serves as a bridge between the earthly self and the celestial energies of the universe. As Starseeds begin to tap into the Cosmic Flame, the practice of meditation becomes even more essential. It offers a sacred space for deep connection, where one can draw from the Cosmic Fire and anchor its transformative power within the soul.

Meditation has been revered across cultures and spiritual

traditions as a path to inner clarity, peace, and higher consciousness. However, Cosmic Flame Meditation goes beyond calming the mind or finding stillness. It actively engages the powerful energies of the Cosmic Flame, which is the divine fire of creation, transformation, and ascension. The Cosmic Flame is not just an ethereal concept but a potent, living energy that resides in the core of every Starseed, waiting to be ignited and expanded.

The Nature of the Cosmic Flame

Before delving into the practice of Cosmic Flame Meditation, it is essential to understand the nature of this sacred fire. The Cosmic Flame is often referred to as the divine spark that connects all beings to the greater universe. It is the essence of the soul's potential, an eternal source of light and energy that powers spiritual evolution. In Starseeds, the Cosmic Flame is more than just a personal energy; it is a direct connection to the cosmic forces that guide and shape the universe.

When a Starseed begins the process of awakening, the Cosmic Flame within them stirs, creating a profound shift in awareness. This awakening process brings with it a realization of the soul's higher purpose and a desire to align with the frequencies of love, unity, and wisdom. Cosmic Flame Meditation is the practice that accelerates this awakening, allowing the Starseed to consciously work with their inner flame to align with their divine mission and the collective ascension of humanity.

Preparing for Cosmic Flame Meditation

The first step in engaging with Cosmic Flame Meditation is preparing the mind, body, and energy field. Unlike other forms of meditation, which may focus solely on mental relaxation, Cosmic Flame Meditation requires the Starseed to be fully grounded and energetically open to receiving higher frequencies.

One of the most important elements in preparation is grounding. Grounding serves as an anchor for the high-frequency energies of the Cosmic Flame, ensuring that the Starseed remains balanced and centered throughout the meditation. Without grounding, the influx of cosmic energies can feel overwhelming, leading to physical or emotional imbalances. Grounding can be achieved through visualization practices, where one envisions roots extending from their body into the earth, or through physical activities such as walking barefoot on the ground.

Another crucial aspect of preparation is clearing the energy field. The Cosmic Flame is pure divine energy, and to fully integrate its power, the Starseed must first clear any energetic blocks or stagnation from their field. This can be done through techniques such as smudging with sage or palo santo, using sound healing tools like tuning forks or singing bowls, or simply engaging in deep breathing exercises that cleanse the body and aura.

Finally, setting a clear intention before beginning the meditation is vital. The Cosmic Flame responds to conscious intent, and by setting an intention to connect with and activate the flame within, the Starseed opens themselves up to deeper levels of transformation and alignment with their soul's purpose.

The Practice of Cosmic Flame Meditation

Once the Starseed has prepared their energy and set their intention, they can move into the actual practice of Cosmic Flame Meditation. This meditation focuses on invoking the Cosmic Flame and bringing it into alignment with the heart, mind, and soul. It is a process of consciously expanding the flame within to connect with the infinite divine fire of the cosmos.

To begin, find a comfortable seated position, either on the floor or in a chair, with the spine straight and the hands resting gently on the knees or in the lap. Close your eyes and take several deep, slow breaths, allowing the body to relax and the mind to settle. Focus on each inhalation, imagining it as a wave of light that enters the body, filling it with peace and calm. With each exhalation, release any tension or distractions.

Once you feel grounded and centered, shift your awareness to the center of your chest, the heart space. The heart is the seat of the soul, and it is here that the Cosmic Flame burns most brightly. Visualize a small, glowing flame flickering in the center of your heart, radiant and warm. This is your personal connection to the Cosmic Flame, a spark of the divine fire that powers your soul's evolution.

With each breath, see this flame grow brighter and larger, expanding outwards to fill your entire chest. Feel its warmth and energy radiating through your body, reaching down into the earth and up into the cosmos. As the flame expands, affirm silently or aloud: "I am the Cosmic Flame. I am connected to the divine fire of the universe." Allow yourself to fully immerse in the experience of this sacred fire.

After several minutes of connecting with and expanding the flame within, shift your focus to the top of your head, the crown chakra. Visualize a stream of golden light descending from the cosmos, flowing down into your crown and merging with the flame in your heart. This golden light represents the cosmic aspect of the flame, the infinite source of divine energy that fuels your inner flame. As the light merges with the flame in your heart, feel the energy intensify, becoming a radiant sun of light that fills your entire being.

Stay with this visualization for as long as you feel guided, basking in the light and warmth of the Cosmic Flame. As you do, allow any thoughts, emotions, or energies that no longer serve you to be transmuted by the flame. The Cosmic Flame is a powerful tool for transformation, and by inviting it into your energy field, you allow it to burn away any blocks or limitations that stand in the way of your ascension.

Benefits of Cosmic Flame Meditation

The benefits of Cosmic Flame Meditation are profound and far-reaching. On a physical level, this meditation helps to release stress, tension, and energetic blocks, creating a sense of peace and well-being. On an emotional level, it brings clarity, allowing the Starseed to release old patterns of fear, doubt, and limitation and replace them with feelings of love, unity, and empowerment.

Spiritually, the effects of Cosmic Flame Meditation are even more profound. As the Starseed connects with and expands their Cosmic Flame, they align with their soul's highest purpose. This alignment brings greater clarity to their path, revealing new insights and opportunities for spiritual growth. The Cosmic Flame also acts as a protective shield, raising the Starseed's vibration and making them less susceptible to negative energies or lower vibrational influences.

Furthermore, regular practice of Cosmic Flame Meditation helps to accelerate the Starseed's ascension process. By continually working with the Cosmic Flame, the Starseed raises their frequency, activating dormant aspects of their divine potential and opening channels of communication with higher dimensions. This meditation deepens the Starseed's connection to the universe, allowing them to receive guidance and support from their galactic guides, higher self, and the cosmic forces that shape their path.

Integrating the Cosmic Flame into Daily Life

While Cosmic Flame Meditation is a powerful tool for spiritual awakening, its true power lies in its integration into daily life. The practice of expanding and nurturing the Cosmic Flame should not be confined to moments of meditation but should be carried into every aspect of the Starseed's existence.

Each day presents an opportunity to connect with the Cosmic Flame, whether through a brief moment of stillness, a conscious breath, or an intentional affirmation. By regularly checking in with the flame within and allowing its energy to guide thoughts, actions, and decisions, the Starseed can ensure that they remain aligned with their higher purpose, even in the midst of daily challenges.

In moments of difficulty or uncertainty, the Starseed can return to the Cosmic Flame as a source of strength and clarity. The flame within is always available, offering its warmth and guidance. By trusting in this inner fire, the Starseed can navigate the complexities of life with grace, knowing that they are always supported by the infinite divine energy of the cosmos.

The Journey Begins

Cosmic Flame Meditation is the beginning of a transformative journey. It is an invitation to dive deep into the mysteries of the universe, to awaken the divine fire within, and to align with the higher purpose of the soul. Through this practice, Starseeds can unlock the full potential of their Cosmic Flame, accelerating their path to ascension and contributing to the collective awakening of humanity and the Earth.

As you begin your practice of Cosmic Flame Meditation, remember that this journey is uniquely yours. Trust in the guidance of your soul and the divine fire that burns within you. The Cosmic Flame is your key to ascension, and by nurturing it, you ignite the path to your highest self and the infinite possibilities that await.

Cosmic Flame Rituals for Transformation

In the journey of ascension, there comes a time when the

Starseed must move beyond the introductory stages of spiritual awakening and engage in deeper, more transformative practices. While Cosmic Flame Meditation is a foundational practice that opens the gateway to inner connection, intermediate-level rituals allow for a more profound interaction with the divine fire. These rituals are designed not just to connect with the Cosmic Flame but to channel its potent energy into every aspect of the Starseed's life, leading to deep inner transformation and alignment with higher spiritual realms.

The Cosmic Flame is not a static force; it is a dynamic, living energy that evolves with the Starseed's progress. As one advances on their path, the flame becomes a tool for self-transformation, capable of dissolving karmic patterns, healing energetic wounds, and accelerating spiritual evolution. Intermediate rituals involving the Cosmic Flame focus on these transformative aspects, guiding the Starseed through inner alchemy, purification, and energetic realignment.

The Power of Ritual for Transformation

Rituals have long been used in spiritual traditions as powerful methods for invoking divine energies and creating sacred space. They serve as an anchor in the physical realm for metaphysical processes, allowing higher frequencies to manifest and interact with the practitioner. In the context of Cosmic Flame rituals, the primary objective is to work with the fire's transformative properties, inviting the energies of purification, renewal, and ascension to take root within the soul.

Rituals offer structure and intention, helping the Starseed to channel the energy of the Cosmic Flame with precision. Through these rituals, the flame is not merely invoked but becomes a dynamic force that can burn away limitations, dissolve egoic structures, and elevate consciousness to higher planes of existence. By consistently engaging in these practices, the Starseed deepens their connection with the Cosmic Flame and begins to embody its divine qualities.

Preparation for Intermediate Cosmic Flame Rituals

As with any advanced spiritual practice, preparation is key to successfully engaging in Cosmic Flame rituals. Before performing any ritual, it is important to establish a sacred space, cleanse your energy, and focus your intention. This preparation ensures that the energy invoked through the ritual is pure and aligned with the highest good.

Creating a sacred space is essential for focusing the energy of the Cosmic Flame. This can be done by selecting a quiet, undisturbed area where the ritual can take place. Incorporating elements that resonate with the Cosmic Flame, such as candles, crystals, or symbols of fire, can enhance the energy of the space and create a heightened sense of connection.

Cleansing the energy field before the ritual is another critical step. The Cosmic Flame works most effectively when the energy body is clear of blockages and stagnant energy. Practices such as smudging, using sound healing tools, or taking a salt bath can help remove lower energies and create an open, receptive state. Deep breathing and grounding exercises are also important to ensure that the physical and energetic bodies are aligned and balanced.

Finally, setting a clear intention is the foundation of any Cosmic Flame ritual. Whether the intention is to heal emotional wounds, release karmic patterns, or deepen your connection to higher realms, the Cosmic Flame responds to focused intention. By clearly defining the purpose of the ritual, the Starseed opens themselves to receiving the full transformative power of the flame.

The Alchemical Ritual of Purification

One of the most important intermediate rituals involving the

Cosmic Flame is the Alchemical Ritual of Purification. This ritual is designed to purify the soul and energy body by invoking the cleansing power of the flame to burn away impurities, negative energies, and limiting patterns. The purification process is a form of inner alchemy, transforming dense or stagnant energies into light and clarity.

To begin the Alchemical Ritual of Purification, find a quiet space where you will not be disturbed. Light a white or golden candle to symbolize the Cosmic Flame, and place it in front of you. Close your eyes, take several deep breaths, and center your awareness in your heart space. Visualize the Cosmic Flame within your heart, burning brightly and steadily.

As you breathe deeply, allow the flame in your heart to grow larger and more radiant. See it expanding outward, filling your entire body with its light. As the flame expands, affirm your intention for purification, saying something like: "I invoke the Cosmic Flame to purify my mind, body, and soul. Let all that no longer serves my highest good be transformed into light."

Next, visualize the flame moving through your energy field, burning away any darkness, heaviness, or negativity. Feel the flame moving through each of your chakras, clearing and balancing them as it goes. If there are any specific areas of your life or energy where you feel stuck, focus the flame on those areas, allowing it to dissolve blockages and stagnation.

As the flame purifies your energy, feel a sense of lightness and clarity emerging within you. When you feel the process is complete, give thanks to the Cosmic Flame for its transformative power, and allow the candle to continue burning as a symbol of your ongoing purification.

The Ritual of Karmic Release

Karmic patterns can often hinder spiritual growth, acting as unseen forces that shape our thoughts, behaviors, and experiences. These patterns are often the result of unresolved lessons from past lives or current experiences, and they can manifest as recurring challenges or limiting beliefs. The Cosmic Flame holds the power to release these karmic patterns by transmuting their energy and freeing the soul from their influence.

The Ritual of Karmic Release is an intermediate-level ritual designed to identify and release karmic imprints that no longer serve your spiritual evolution. Begin by creating a sacred space and lighting a candle, as in the previous ritual. Sit comfortably, close your eyes, and take several deep breaths to center yourself.

Once you feel grounded, bring your awareness to your heart space and visualize the Cosmic Flame burning brightly within you. As you focus on the flame, ask it to reveal any karmic patterns or lessons that are ready to be released. You may see images, feel sensations, or have thoughts that point to specific areas of your life where karmic energy is present.

When you have identified a karmic pattern, visualize the flame expanding to encompass the energy of that pattern. See the flame surrounding the karmic energy, dissolving it and transforming it into light. As the flame works, affirm that you are releasing this karmic imprint, saying something like: "I release this karmic pattern with love and gratitude. I transmute its energy into light and align with my highest path."

Continue this process with any other karmic patterns that come to mind. When you feel the ritual is complete, express gratitude to the Cosmic Flame for its assistance, and allow the candle to burn out naturally. This ritual can be repeated as needed to address ongoing karmic patterns that arise in your life.

The Ritual of Empowerment and Manifestation

The Cosmic Flame is not only a tool for healing and release; it is also a powerful force for manifestation. By aligning with the divine energies of the flame, the Starseed can use its power to create and manifest higher realities. The Ritual of Empowerment and Manifestation is designed to focus the energy of the Cosmic Flame on specific goals or intentions, bringing them into physical reality.

To begin the ritual, create a sacred space and light a candle, as in the previous rituals. Sit comfortably and take several deep breaths to center yourself. Bring your awareness to your heart space and visualize the Cosmic Flame burning brightly within you.

Next, focus on the intention or goal you wish to manifest. This could be related to your spiritual growth, personal development, or a specific area of your life where you seek transformation. Hold this intention in your mind and see it surrounded by the light of the Cosmic Flame.

As you focus on your intention, visualize the Cosmic Flame expanding to encompass it. See the flame growing larger and brighter, filling your entire energy field with its light. Affirm that the Cosmic Flame is empowering your intention, saying something like: "I align with the Cosmic Flame and its divine power to manifest my highest intentions. I am empowered by the flame to create the reality I desire."

Feel the energy of the flame growing stronger, infusing your intention with divine power. As the flame works, trust that your intention is being manifested in alignment with the highest good. When you feel the process is complete, express gratitude to the Cosmic Flame, and allow the candle to continue burning as a symbol of your empowered intention.

Embracing the Power of Transformation

Intermediate Cosmic Flame rituals offer profound opportunities for transformation, allowing the Starseed to engage more deeply with the divine fire within. Through purification, karmic release, and manifestation, these rituals facilitate a deeper connection with the Cosmic Flame and accelerate the process of ascension. As the Starseed continues to work with these rituals, they will experience ongoing growth, empowerment, and alignment with their soul's highest purpose.

By embracing the power of the Cosmic Flame, the Starseed steps into a new phase of their spiritual journey, one that is marked by greater clarity, purpose, and transformation. The flame within is a constant source of guidance, healing, and empowerment, and through these rituals, its light will continue to grow, illuminating the path ahead.

Manifesting with the Cosmic Fire

Manifestation is the process of bringing forth desires, visions, or intentions from the realm of thought and energy into tangible reality. For Starseeds, who are naturally attuned to the cosmic vibrations, the act of manifestation becomes a sacred co-creative process with the universe. It is here, within the intricate dance between spirit and matter, that the Cosmic Fire plays an essential role. The Cosmic Flame, the universal force that fuels spiritual ascension, holds within it the divine power to transmute thoughts into reality, enabling Starseeds to consciously craft their lives in alignment with higher purposes.

Manifesting with the Cosmic Fire is far more than the pursuit of material desires; it is about aligning one's soul mission with the greater energies of the cosmos. The key to working with the

Cosmic Flame for manifestation lies in understanding its higher vibrational frequency, learning to tap into it, and channeling that energy into clear, focused intentions.

The Cosmic Flame and the Laws of Manifestation

At the core of manifestation lies the universal Law of Attraction, which states that like attracts like. Thoughts, emotions, and beliefs are vibrational frequencies that interact with the universe. The energy you send out—through your mental and emotional patterns—returns to you in the form of experiences, relationships, and circumstances that match that vibration.

The Cosmic Flame enhances this process by infusing your intentions with its divine power. While the Law of Attraction works through personal vibrational alignment, the Cosmic Flame magnifies and accelerates the manifestation process by raising the frequency of your desires to a higher vibrational level. When you invoke the Cosmic Fire, you are tapping into a divine source of creation that transcends individual will and aligns with the collective, universal will.

However, to manifest with the Cosmic Flame, it is crucial to be in alignment with your soul's highest path. The energy of the flame is pure and works in concert with the evolution of the soul. If the intention behind your manifestation is driven by ego or materialistic cravings, the Cosmic Flame may not respond, as its primary function is to facilitate spiritual growth and ascension. The key to successful manifestation with the Cosmic Fire lies in surrendering personal will to divine will, trusting that what is in alignment with the highest good will unfold in perfect timing.

Tapping into the Cosmic Flame for Manifestation

Manifesting with the Cosmic Fire requires more than setting a clear intention; it involves entering into a sacred space of co-creation where the Starseed merges their personal energy field with the cosmic forces at play. This is done through a combination of meditation, visualization, and ritual, all of which focus on aligning one's inner energy with the vibrational frequency of the Cosmic Flame.

Before beginning any manifestation work, it is essential to purify your energy field. Negative emotions, limiting beliefs, and energetic blockages can interfere with the manifestation process by lowering your vibrational frequency. Engaging in regular practices of energy cleansing—such as smudging with sacred herbs, taking a salt bath, or using sound healing—helps prepare your energetic body for the high vibrational work of manifestation.

Once your energy is clear, the next step is to enter a meditative state where you can attune yourself to the Cosmic Flame. Visualize the flame burning within your heart center, expanding with each breath you take. Feel its warmth, light, and transformative power as it fills your entire being, raising your vibrational frequency. As you connect with the flame, allow yourself to enter a state of gratitude and openness, recognizing that you are a co-creator with the universe, capable of manifesting your highest intentions through divine partnership.

Visualization: Bridging Energy and Matter

One of the most powerful tools for manifestation is visualization. This practice bridges the gap between the energetic realm of thoughts and the physical realm of matter. When you visualize something with clarity and focus, you are creating a blueprint for that reality in the energetic realm. By holding that vision in alignment with the Cosmic Flame, you magnify its vibrational frequency, allowing it to more easily take shape in the physical world.

Begin by clearly defining what you wish to manifest. Whether it is a specific goal, a state of being, or a life circumstance, ensure that your intention is aligned with your soul's higher purpose.

Once you have defined your intention, enter your meditative state and visualize your desire as if it has already manifested. Imagine every detail: what it looks like, how it feels, the emotions associated with it, and how it impacts your life and those around you.

As you visualize, see the Cosmic Flame surrounding your intention, infusing it with divine light and power. Feel the flame burning away any doubts or fears that may arise, purifying your desire so that it is in alignment with your soul's highest path. The more vividly and consistently you can hold this vision in your mind's eye, the more energy you are directing toward its manifestation.

Ritual: Empowering Intentions with the Cosmic Flame

Ritual plays a crucial role in manifestation because it grounds the energetic work into the physical realm. The act of creating a ritual with the Cosmic Flame allows the Starseed to anchor the divine energy into their daily life, creating a bridge between the spiritual and material worlds. Rituals bring a tangible, sensory aspect to the manifestation process, which strengthens the connection between intention and reality.

A manifestation ritual with the Cosmic Flame begins by creating a sacred space where you can connect with the divine energies. Light a candle to represent the Cosmic Flame, and gather items that symbolize your intention, such as crystals, herbs, or written affirmations. These items act as energetic conduits, amplifying your intention and connecting it to the higher frequencies of the flame.

Once your sacred space is prepared, enter into meditation and connect with the Cosmic Flame within your heart. Hold your intention clearly in your mind, and as you focus on it, visualize the flame surrounding it, empowering it with divine energy. As you perform the ritual, whether through lighting the candle, speaking affirmations aloud, or making symbolic gestures, allow yourself to fully surrender to the process, trusting that the Cosmic Flame is working in alignment with the universal will to bring your desire into manifestation.

Rituals can be repeated regularly to reinforce the energy of your intention, creating a consistent flow of cosmic energy toward your goal. The key is to remain patient and trust in divine timing. While the manifestation may not happen immediately, each ritual adds more energy to the process, allowing the universe to work in harmony with your desire.

Surrender and Trust: The Final Step in Manifestation

Perhaps the most challenging yet essential aspect of manifesting with the Cosmic Flame is the practice of surrender. While it is important to set clear intentions and engage in rituals, the ultimate act of manifestation requires the Starseed to let go of attachment to the outcome. This is where faith and trust in the universe come into play.

The Cosmic Flame operates according to the laws of divine timing and alignment. Sometimes, what we desire may not come to fruition in the way we expect or within the timeline we envision. This does not mean that the flame is not working; rather, it is a reminder that the universe is constantly orchestrating events in perfect harmony for the highest good of all. Trusting in this process is crucial for manifestation to unfold with ease.

After you have set your intention and performed your rituals, release your desire into the universe with faith and gratitude. Know that the Cosmic Flame is working on your behalf, even if you cannot yet see the results. By surrendering attachment to the outcome, you allow the divine energies to flow more freely, opening the door for miracles to manifest in ways beyond your imagination.

Manifesting Collective Transformation

While much of manifestation work focuses on individual desires and goals, Starseeds have a unique role in manifesting collective transformation. As channels for the Cosmic Flame, Starseeds are called to use their powers of manifestation not only for personal growth but also for the evolution of humanity and the planet.

Through collective rituals, global meditations, and intentional community-building, Starseeds can harness the Cosmic Flame to manifest positive change on a larger scale. Whether it is through healing the Earth, raising the collective consciousness, or facilitating peace and unity, the Cosmic Flame offers infinite possibilities for creating a more harmonious world.

By working with the Cosmic Flame in this way, Starseeds become co-creators of a new reality, one that is aligned with the principles of love, compassion, and ascension. In this sacred work, the personal and collective become one, and the Cosmic Flame serves as the bridge between the two, manifesting the highest vision for all.

Manifesting with the Cosmic Fire is a sacred art that requires alignment, intention, and trust. By tapping into the divine power of the Cosmic Flame, Starseeds can co-create their realities in harmony with the universe's highest will. Whether manifesting personal desires or contributing to collective transformation, the Cosmic Flame empowers Starseeds to bring their visions into reality, making them active participants in the cosmic dance of creation.

In embracing this role, Starseeds not only fulfill their soul's purpose but also contribute to the ascension of humanity and the Earth, helping to anchor a new reality filled with light, love, and divine harmony.

Advanced Cosmic Flame Mastery Rituals

In the vast journey of spiritual awakening and ascension, the Cosmic Flame stands as a profound tool for transformation, purification, and empowerment. As Starseeds evolve in their spiritual practice, mastering the Cosmic Flame becomes an essential element in transcending the limitations of the material world and fully embodying the wisdom of higher dimensions. Advanced Cosmic Flame rituals offer a gateway into this mastery, providing methods for Starseeds to work consciously with this sacred energy to achieve deeper spiritual breakthroughs.

Mastery of the Cosmic Flame is more than just intellectual understanding or casual practice—it is an integration of the flame's transformative power into every aspect of one's being. Through advanced rituals, the Cosmic Flame can be wielded to dissolve remaining karmic imprints, unlock latent spiritual gifts, and activate profound energetic shifts within the self and the collective consciousness. These rituals require dedication, heightened awareness, and an unwavering intention to align with the highest frequencies of the Cosmic Flame.

The Sacred Commitment to Mastery

Mastering the Cosmic Flame demands more than a desire for personal advancement; it requires a commitment to embodying higher consciousness in daily life. For Starseeds on this path, it means surrendering the ego's need for control and allowing the Cosmic Flame to flow through them as a divine instrument. This surrender is not passive but an active, conscious choice to become a vessel for cosmic energy. The Cosmic Flame thrives in an environment of trust, faith, and purity of intention.

One of the first steps in this process is recognizing the difference between control and mastery. Control implies an attempt to dictate the outcome, whereas mastery allows the natural flow of the Cosmic Flame to work in perfect harmony with divine will.

A Starseed aligned with mastery understands that the Cosmic Flame has its own intelligence and operates on a frequency far beyond personal desires. Therefore, advanced rituals often begin with a profound act of surrender, in which the Starseed offers their energy field to the Cosmic Flame, trusting that it will facilitate the highest good for all involved.

The Power of Intention and Focus

At the heart of every advanced ritual is the clarity of intention. When working with the Cosmic Flame, intention becomes the bridge between the energetic realm and the material world. For advanced practitioners, the role of intention is elevated beyond personal goals to include the collective consciousness. Intentions may focus on global healing, planetary ascension, or the activation of the light grid. In these instances, the Cosmic Flame acts as both an individual and collective force of transformation, aligning personal evolution with the ascension of humanity and Earth.

Focus is equally critical in advanced Cosmic Flame rituals. As a practitioner deepens their work with the flame, the mind must be trained to remain steady and clear. Distractions, doubts, and mental chatter dilute the energy of the ritual. In advanced practice, the Starseed learns to enter into a state of deep mental stillness, where the mind, body, and spirit are fully aligned. This heightened focus amplifies the power of the Cosmic Flame, allowing it to penetrate deeper into the energetic layers of the practitioner and the surrounding environment.

Ritual of Karmic Liberation with the Cosmic Flame

One of the most powerful uses of the Cosmic Flame in advanced rituals is the liberation from karmic imprints. These imprints —energetic patterns from past lifetimes—can hinder the soul's progression toward full ascension. While basic rituals may focus on healing surface-level imprints, advanced rituals address the deeper layers of karma that often remain hidden in the subconscious or subtle energy bodies.

To perform a ritual of karmic liberation, begin by creating a sacred space. Light a candle to represent the Cosmic Flame, and surround yourself with objects that hold high vibrational energy, such as crystals or sacred symbols. Sit in meditation and focus on your breath, allowing your mind to become still. Once you feel centered, visualize the Cosmic Flame within your heart, expanding with each breath.

With clear intention, call upon the Cosmic Flame to illuminate any karmic imprints that are ready to be released. As these imprints come into your awareness—whether they appear as images, emotions, or physical sensations—breathe into them, and allow the flame to burn through the karmic residue. Visualize the flame dissolving the imprint entirely, transmuting its energy into light. Continue this process for as long as needed, trusting that the Cosmic Flame is guiding you toward full liberation.

This ritual may need to be repeated multiple times, as some karmic imprints are deeply rooted and require ongoing work to fully clear. However, with each ritual, you will feel a sense of lightness and freedom, as the soul is progressively freed from the bonds of past karma.

Planetary Healing Ritual with the Cosmic Flame

As Starseeds advance in their mastery of the Cosmic Flame, they become powerful conduits for planetary healing. The Cosmic Flame has the unique ability to heal not only individuals but also collective energies, making it a crucial tool for those who wish to contribute to global ascension. In planetary healing rituals, the focus shifts from personal transformation to collective liberation, with the Cosmic Flame being directed toward the Earth and humanity as a whole.

To begin a planetary healing ritual, enter into a meditative state and connect with the Cosmic Flame within your heart. Visualize the flame expanding outward, growing in size and intensity until it envelops your entire body. As the flame continues to grow, see it expanding beyond your physical space, until it surrounds the Earth in a cocoon of light. Hold the vision of the Earth completely bathed in the Cosmic Flame, and set the intention for the healing of the planet and all sentient beings.

As you maintain this visualization, focus on specific areas that need healing—whether it be regions of conflict, environmental devastation, or collective suffering. Direct the energy of the Cosmic Flame toward these areas, visualizing it transmuting dense energies and restoring balance. This ritual can be performed alone or in groups, with the combined energy of multiple Starseeds amplifying the power of the flame. As you conclude the ritual, express gratitude to the Cosmic Flame for its healing presence, and trust that the energy you have directed will continue to work in alignment with the highest good.

The Role of the Higher Self in Cosmic Flame Mastery

In advanced Cosmic Flame rituals, the role of the Higher Self becomes increasingly significant. The Higher Self is the aspect of the soul that exists beyond the limitations of the material world and is fully attuned to the Cosmic Flame's frequency. To truly master the Cosmic Flame, Starseeds must cultivate a deep connection with their Higher Self, allowing it to guide their actions, intentions, and energy work.

One advanced technique for strengthening the connection with the Higher Self is through direct invocation during Cosmic Flame rituals. Before beginning the ritual, call upon your Higher Self to join you in the sacred space. Visualize your Higher Self as a radiant being of light, standing beside you or merging with your energy field. As you work with the Cosmic Flame, allow your Higher Self to take the lead, trusting that it knows how to direct the energy for the highest possible outcome.

Working with the Higher Self in this way elevates the ritual from a personal practice to a cosmic co-creation. The Higher Self operates beyond the confines of time, space, and ego, allowing for a deeper and more profound interaction with the Cosmic Flame. Through this partnership, the Starseed becomes a pure channel for divine energy, capable of manifesting extraordinary shifts in both personal and planetary consciousness.

Advanced mastery of the Cosmic Flame requires dedication, intention, and an unwavering connection to the higher realms of consciousness. Through rituals of karmic liberation, planetary healing, and deep communion with the Higher Self, Starseeds can unlock the full potential of the Cosmic Flame, using its transformative power to facilitate ascension on all levels. These advanced rituals are not merely practices of personal development—they are acts of cosmic service, aligning the individual with the greater mission of global and universal awakening.

In embracing this sacred work, Starseeds become masters of the Cosmic Flame, co-creating a reality of light, love, and divine harmony. Through their mastery, they contribute to the ascension of all beings, fulfilling their soul's highest purpose and embodying the true essence of the Cosmic Flame in every aspect of their existence.

THE STARSEED LIGHT BODY ACTIVATION

Understanding the Light Body

The light body is an essential aspect of the Starseed's ascension journey, representing a higher vibrational state of being that transcends the limitations of physical matter. As Starseeds evolve and attune to the cosmic frequencies of the universe, the light body becomes their primary vehicle for navigating higher dimensions, accessing divine wisdom, and anchoring higher consciousness on Earth. Understanding the light body is crucial for those seeking to reach the highest levels of spiritual mastery, as it is both the key to personal ascension and a bridge to the collective evolution of humanity.

The light body is not simply a metaphysical concept but a

multidimensional structure made up of various layers of energy. It serves as the interface between the soul and the physical body, allowing Starseeds to channel cosmic energy into the material realm. Activating the light body allows for expanded states of awareness, greater alignment with the soul's purpose, and the capacity to hold and transmit higher frequencies of love, light, and healing.

The Multidimensional Nature of the Light Body

The light body exists beyond the confines of the third-dimensional physical reality. It operates within higher dimensions, including the fourth, fifth, and beyond. In essence, it is a vibrational blueprint that carries the codes of the soul's evolution and holds the potential for infinite expansion. As Starseeds begin to awaken to their cosmic origins, their light body becomes more active, responding to the influx of higher frequencies from the universe.

The light body consists of several layers, each corresponding to different aspects of consciousness and spiritual growth. These layers, often referred to as the subtle bodies, include the etheric, emotional, mental, and spiritual bodies. Together, they form the energetic field that surrounds and permeates the physical body, known as the aura. As Starseeds progress on their ascension journey, these layers become more refined and integrated, allowing for greater harmony between the physical, emotional, mental, and spiritual aspects of the self.

The light body also serves as a vessel for cosmic energy, acting as a conduit through which divine light and wisdom flow. This energy is absorbed through various energy centers, or chakras, which are aligned with the physical and etheric bodies. When the light body is activated, these chakras open to receive higher frequencies, allowing the Starseed to embody higher states of consciousness and align more fully with their soul's purpose. The light body is not static but a dynamic and evolving system that grows in strength and luminosity as the individual engages in spiritual practices and connects with higher realms of consciousness.

The Role of the Light Body in Ascension

The light body plays a fundamental role in the ascension process. As Starseeds awaken to their higher selves and connect with the Cosmic Flame, their light body becomes the vehicle through which they ascend to higher dimensions. This process of ascension involves raising the vibration of the physical, emotional, and mental bodies to match the frequencies of the light body. When these frequencies are in harmony, the individual experiences an expanded state of consciousness and a deeper connection to the divine.

In practical terms, the activation of the light body allows Starseeds to access higher wisdom, heal karmic imprints, and manifest their soul's purpose with greater clarity and ease. The light body acts as a bridge between the material and spiritual realms, facilitating communication with higher beings, including galactic guides, ascended masters, and other celestial entities. It is through the light body that Starseeds can travel interdimensionally, receive divine guidance, and anchor higher frequencies of light into the Earth's energy grid.

As the light body becomes more active, it also serves as a tool for personal and planetary healing. The high-frequency energy channeled through the light body has the power to transmute lower vibrational energies, heal physical and emotional imbalances, and raise the collective vibration of humanity. In this way, the light body is not only essential for individual ascension but also plays a critical role in the global shift toward higher consciousness.

Activating the Light Body

The activation of the light body is a gradual process that

unfolds as the individual raises their vibration and aligns more fully with their higher self. While the light body is always present, it may remain dormant or inactive if the individual is not consciously engaged in spiritual practices that support its activation. However, once the Starseed begins to work with higher frequencies, such as the Cosmic Flame, and engages in practices that elevate their consciousness, the light body naturally begins to awaken.

One of the most effective ways to activate the light body is through meditation. Meditation allows the individual to enter into a state of deep relaxation and attunement, where they can consciously connect with the higher frequencies of the universe. By focusing on the breath and visualizing the light body expanding and becoming more luminous, the Starseed can begin to activate the energy centers and open the channels through which cosmic energy flows.

Another powerful tool for light body activation is the use of sacred symbols and geometry. These symbols carry specific frequencies that resonate with the light body and can help to unlock dormant energies within the individual. For example, the Merkaba, a sacred geometric symbol, is often used in light body activation practices. This symbol represents the vehicle of ascension and is believed to activate the light body's ability to travel interdimensionally.

Additionally, working with the Cosmic Flame is essential for light body activation. The Cosmic Flame is a divine energy that burns away lower vibrational energies and purifies the individual's energy field. By invoking the Cosmic Flame and visualizing it merging with the light body, the Starseed can accelerate the process of activation and enhance their connection to higher dimensions.

Supporting the Light Body Through Physical and Energetic Practices

While the activation of the light body is primarily an energetic process, it is also important to support this process through physical practices that align the body with higher frequencies. The physical body is the vessel through which the light body operates, and maintaining its health and vitality is essential for sustaining the higher vibrations of the light body.

One way to support the light body is through nutrition. Eating high-vibrational foods, such as fresh fruits, vegetables, and whole grains, provides the body with the nutrients it needs to maintain its energy and vitality. Additionally, drinking plenty of water and staying hydrated is important for keeping the energy channels open and allowing the light body to function at its highest capacity.

Another important practice for supporting the light body is regular physical movement. Activities such as yoga, tai chi, and qigong help to balance the energy centers, strengthen the connection between the physical and energetic bodies, and promote the flow of cosmic energy throughout the system. These practices also help to release any blockages or stagnant energy that may be preventing the full activation of the light body.

In addition to physical practices, it is important to engage in regular energy work to support the light body. Practices such as Reiki, energy healing, and working with crystals can help to clear the energy field, balance the chakras, and strengthen the light body's connection to higher frequencies. By incorporating these practices into daily life, the Starseed can maintain the health and vitality of their light body and continue to expand their consciousness on the path to ascension.

The light body is a sacred and multidimensional aspect of the Starseed's being, representing their connection to higher realms and their potential for ascension. As the Starseed activates and strengthens their light body, they open themselves to new levels of spiritual awareness, healing, and transformation. The light body is not only a tool for personal evolution but also a vehicle for planetary healing and the collective ascension of humanity.

By understanding the light body and engaging in practices that support its activation, Starseeds can unlock their full potential and step into their roles as divine beings of light. Through meditation, energy work, and physical practices, they can maintain the health and vitality of their light body and continue to ascend to higher levels of consciousness. As the light body becomes more active, the Starseed becomes a beacon of light for others, guiding humanity toward a brighter and more harmonious future.

Preparing the Physical Body for Light Integration

As Starseeds embark on the path of ascension, the transformation is not limited to the spiritual and energetic realms. The physical body, often overlooked in its profound role within the spiritual journey, becomes a crucial vessel in this process. Preparing the physical body for light integration is essential for supporting the activation and sustenance of the light body, a multidimensional energetic system that serves as a bridge to higher consciousness. Without adequate preparation and care, the physical body may struggle to hold the high-frequency energies necessary for ascension, leading to imbalances and disruptions that hinder the journey.

The Physical Body as a Sacred Temple

The physical body is a divine creation, intricately designed to support the soul's journey on Earth. In many spiritual traditions, the body is regarded as a temple—a sacred space where the soul resides. For Starseeds, this concept takes on even greater significance, as their physical form is not merely a vessel for earthly experiences, but a conduit for cosmic energies and ascension.

As the body integrates higher frequencies, it undergoes subtle yet profound changes. These shifts can manifest as sensations of lightness, increased sensitivity, or even physical discomfort as old energies are purged and higher vibrations take root. It is essential to honor and support the body during this process, recognizing that the physical self plays a key role in the overall spiritual journey. Without the foundation of a healthy, balanced body, the light body cannot be fully activated or sustained.

The more Starseeds connect with their physical selves, the more they realize that the body is not separate from their spiritual evolution. It is, in fact, an integral aspect of their ascension, requiring the same level of care, attention, and nurturing as the soul and the mind. By creating a harmonious relationship between the physical and spiritual aspects of their being, Starseeds can facilitate a smoother and more profound integration of light.

Nutrition as an Energetic Foundation

One of the most effective ways to support the physical body during light integration is through mindful nutrition. The food we consume directly influences our energy levels, vitality, and overall frequency. Just as low-vibrational foods can weigh down the body and block energy flow, high-vibrational foods can uplift and energize the system, making it easier to integrate higher frequencies of light.

For Starseeds, the ideal diet consists of foods that are as close to their natural state as possible. Fresh fruits and vegetables, whole grains, nuts, seeds, and legumes provide the body with essential nutrients and high-vibrational energy. These foods are rich in life force energy, or prana, which enhances the body's ability to align with the frequencies of the light body.

In addition to incorporating more plant-based foods into their diet, Starseeds may benefit from reducing or eliminating foods that lower their vibration. Processed foods, refined sugars, and artificial additives can create energetic blockages in the body, making it more difficult to maintain a high frequency. By choosing whole, nutrient-dense foods, Starseeds can fuel their bodies with the energy needed to support their spiritual journey.

Hydration is another key component of maintaining high energy levels. Water is not only essential for physical health but also plays a crucial role in energy flow and detoxification. By staying adequately hydrated, Starseeds can help their bodies release toxins, clear energy blockages, and enhance the flow of light throughout their system. Drinking pure, filtered water, and incorporating hydrating foods like cucumbers and watermelon, can further support this process.

Movement as a Pathway for Energy Flow

In addition to nutrition, regular physical movement is essential for preparing the body to integrate higher frequencies of light. Movement helps to stimulate energy flow, release stagnant energy, and create space within the body for new, higher vibrations to enter. It also strengthens the physical body, making it more resilient and capable of holding light.

For Starseeds, gentle, mindful forms of movement such as yoga, tai chi, and qigong are particularly beneficial. These practices focus on the flow of energy, or chi, through the body's meridians and energy centers. By practicing these movements regularly, Starseeds can keep their energy channels open and balanced, ensuring that the Cosmic Flame and other high-frequency energies can flow freely through their system.

Yoga, in particular, is a powerful tool for preparing the body for light integration. The various asanas, or postures, help to stretch and strengthen the muscles, increase flexibility, and promote relaxation. In addition, the practice of pranayama, or breath control, helps to oxygenate the body and enhance the flow of prana, the life force energy. By combining movement with conscious breathing, yoga allows Starseeds to create a deeper connection between their physical and energetic bodies, facilitating a smoother integration of light.

Incorporating regular movement into daily life can also help to release emotional and energetic blockages that may be stored in the body. As the body moves and stretches, it releases tension and stagnant energy, allowing for greater clarity and flow. Whether through yoga, dance, walking, or other forms of physical activity, movement is a vital part of maintaining the health and vitality of the physical body during the ascension process.

Energy Practices to Support Light Integration

In addition to physical movement, energy work is a crucial component of preparing the body for light integration. Practices such as Reiki, acupuncture, and sound healing can help to balance the body's energy centers, clear blockages, and support the flow of light throughout the system.

Reiki, for example, is a form of energy healing that works with the body's natural energy flow. By channeling universal life force energy, Reiki practitioners can help to release blockages, balance the chakras, and restore harmony to the body. This practice is particularly beneficial for Starseeds who are integrating higher frequencies, as it helps to clear any lower vibrational energies that may be hindering the flow of light.

Sound healing is another powerful tool for supporting light integration. Sound has a profound effect on the body, mind, and spirit, and certain frequencies are known to resonate with specific chakras and energy centers. By using sound healing instruments such as singing bowls, tuning forks, and gongs, Starseeds can attune their bodies to higher frequencies and facilitate the flow of light through their system. The vibrations of sound can help to release blockages, balance the energy centers, and promote deep relaxation and healing.

Incorporating these energy practices into regular self-care

routines can help Starseeds maintain the health and vitality of their physical and energetic bodies. By clearing blockages, balancing the chakras, and enhancing the flow of energy, these practices create an environment where the body can more easily integrate higher frequencies of light.

Rest and Self-Care as Sacred Practices

Finally, it is essential for Starseeds to honor their need for rest and self-care during the process of light integration. The physical body undergoes significant changes as it integrates higher frequencies, and this can be physically and energetically demanding. It is important to recognize when the body needs rest and to create space for relaxation and rejuvenation.

Self-care practices such as meditation, deep breathing, and spending time in nature can help to calm the nervous system, reduce stress, and promote healing. By creating a sacred space for rest and relaxation, Starseeds can support their bodies in integrating light and maintaining a high frequency.

Sleep is also a vital component of self-care during light integration. During sleep, the body undergoes repair and regeneration, and the light body continues to integrate higher frequencies. Ensuring that the body receives adequate rest is crucial for maintaining the energy and vitality needed for the ascension process.

Preparing the physical body for light integration is a holistic process that involves nurturing the body through mindful nutrition, movement, energy work, and self-care. By creating a harmonious relationship between the physical and energetic bodies, Starseeds can support the flow of light and enhance their ability to anchor higher frequencies on Earth. The body is a sacred temple, and when treated with care and respect, it becomes a powerful vehicle for ascension and spiritual growth.

Activating the Light Body with the Cosmic Flame

The journey toward ascension involves not only the evolution of consciousness but also the transformation of the physical and energetic bodies. Central to this process is the activation of the light body, an advanced energetic structure that allows Starseeds to transcend the limitations of the physical realm and align more deeply with the higher dimensions. The light body is a multidimensional field of energy that, when activated, connects the individual to the cosmic source, enhancing their spiritual capabilities and elevating their vibrational frequency.

Activating the light body is a profound milestone in the Starseed's journey. It signifies the merging of the physical, emotional, mental, and spiritual aspects of the self into a cohesive, higher-frequency state. By working with the Cosmic Flame, Starseeds can accelerate the awakening of their light body, clearing energetic blockages, enhancing their connection to the divine, and preparing for the full embodiment of ascension.

Understanding the Light Body

The light body is often described as the vehicle for ascension, an ethereal structure that surrounds the physical body and expands into higher-dimensional planes of existence. This body of light is composed of high-frequency energy that vibrates at a level beyond the physical, and its activation enables the individual to access spiritual gifts, enhance intuitive abilities, and align with their divine purpose.

In its dormant state, the light body is present within every individual, but it remains inactive until certain spiritual milestones are reached. For Starseeds, the activation of the light body is a key aspect of their mission on Earth, as it allows them to anchor higher energies into the planet and contribute to the collective ascension. This activation process involves the awakening of dormant DNA codes, the purification of the energy body, and the alignment of the individual with their higher self and the divine cosmic blueprint.

The activation of the light body is often accompanied by profound shifts in consciousness, as well as physical, emotional, and energetic changes. Starseeds may experience heightened sensitivity to energy, increased intuitive abilities, and a deepened connection to their soul purpose. As the light body awakens, the individual becomes more attuned to the multidimensional aspects of their being, able to navigate higher realms of consciousness and interact with cosmic energies in a more direct and conscious way.

The Role of the Cosmic Flame in Light Body Activation

The Cosmic Flame is a powerful universal force of transmutation and transformation that has long been associated with spiritual awakening and ascension. It is the divine spark that ignites the process of soul evolution, burning away lower vibrational energies and illuminating the path toward higher states of consciousness. When used consciously in the process of light body activation, the Cosmic Flame acts as a catalyst, accelerating the awakening of the higher self and facilitating the integration of light into the physical and energetic bodies.

The Cosmic Flame has the unique ability to dissolve energetic blockages, clear karmic patterns, and purify the emotional, mental, and spiritual bodies. This purification process is essential for the activation of the light body, as it removes the dense, lower vibrational energies that may prevent the full expression of the higher self. By working with the Cosmic Flame, Starseeds can release old energies, align with their soul's highest potential, and create the energetic space necessary for the light body to emerge.

To activate the light body using the Cosmic Flame, it is important to engage in consistent spiritual practices that align the individual with this powerful energy. Meditation, visualization, and energy work are all effective tools for connecting with the Cosmic Flame and facilitating the awakening of the light body. These practices allow the individual to raise their vibration, clear blockages, and anchor higher frequencies of light into their being.

Meditation for Light Body Activation

Meditation is one of the most powerful practices for activating the light body, as it creates the inner space necessary for higher frequencies to enter the physical and energetic bodies. Through focused intention and deep relaxation, Starseeds can open themselves to the Cosmic Flame, allowing its purifying energy to flow through their system and awaken their light body.

In a typical meditation for light body activation, the Starseed begins by grounding their energy, connecting with the Earth, and visualizing their physical body surrounded by light. They then call upon the Cosmic Flame, inviting its transformative energy to flow through their entire being. This energy is often visualized as a brilliant, radiant flame, filling the body with light and dissolving any blockages or lower vibrational energies.

As the Cosmic Flame moves through the body, the Starseed may focus on specific areas where they feel tension or resistance, allowing the flame to clear and purify these areas. Once the body is fully enveloped in the Cosmic Flame, the focus shifts to the light body, visualizing it as a radiant field of energy surrounding the physical form. By holding this image and intention, the Starseed can facilitate the activation of their light body, inviting its higher frequencies to integrate into their physical and energetic systems.

This meditation can be repeated regularly, allowing the Starseed to deepen their connection with the Cosmic Flame and further activate their light body over time. With practice, the light body becomes more active and integrated, enhancing the individual's ability to connect with higher realms and embody their soul's purpose on Earth.

Clearing Blockages and Aligning with Higher Frequencies

In order to fully activate the light body, it is essential to clear any energetic blockages or lower vibrational energies that may be preventing the free flow of light. These blockages can exist in the form of emotional wounds, limiting beliefs, or karmic patterns that have accumulated over lifetimes. The Cosmic Flame, with its purifying energy, can be used to dissolve these blockages and create the space necessary for the light body to emerge.

Working with the Cosmic Flame involves a process of deep inner healing, where Starseeds consciously address the areas of their life that are out of alignment with their highest truth. This may involve releasing old patterns of fear, guilt, or shame, and embracing a higher vibration of love, compassion, and self-acceptance. By clearing these blockages, the Starseed can raise their vibration and align with the frequencies of their light body, allowing its energy to fully integrate into their being.

In addition to clearing blockages, it is important for Starseeds to consistently align themselves with higher frequencies of light. This can be achieved through spiritual practices such as prayer, affirmation, and visualization, where the individual consciously connects with their higher self and invites divine light into their life. By maintaining a high vibrational state, the Starseed can support the continued activation and expansion of their light body, allowing them to embody higher states of consciousness and fulfill their soul's mission on Earth.

Integration of the Light Body into Daily Life

Once the light body is activated, the journey is not complete —it is an ongoing process of integration, where the Starseed learns to live in alignment with their higher self and embody the energies of their light body in their daily life. This requires a commitment to spiritual growth and self-awareness, as well as a willingness to release old habits, beliefs, and patterns that are no longer in alignment with the higher frequencies of light.

As the light body becomes more active, the individual may notice significant changes in their perception, intuition, and spiritual abilities. They may experience heightened sensitivity to energy, deeper intuitive insights, and a greater sense of connection to the divine. These shifts are all signs of the light body's activation, and they serve as a reminder of the individual's progress on the path of ascension.

To fully integrate the light body, it is important for Starseeds to remain grounded and balanced in their daily life. This can be achieved through regular spiritual practices, mindful self-care, and a conscious connection with the Earth. By maintaining this balance, the Starseed can continue to expand their light body and align with the higher frequencies of the Cosmic Flame, creating a harmonious flow of energy that supports their ascension journey.

Activating the light body with the Cosmic Flame is a transformative process that requires dedication, spiritual practice, and inner healing. By working with this powerful energy, Starseeds can awaken their light body, clear energetic blockages, and align with the higher frequencies of light necessary for ascension. The light body is a gateway to higher consciousness, and its activation represents a significant step on the journey toward full spiritual awakening and mastery.

Mastering the Light Body for Full Ascension

The concept of mastering the light body is not just an abstract spiritual goal but a profound transformation that represents the full embodiment of higher consciousness within the human form. For Starseeds, this mastery is a pivotal step toward full ascension, enabling them to integrate the higher realms into the physical plane and exist as bridges between worlds. The light body, often described as the vehicle for ascension, is the energetic matrix through which spiritual consciousness is translated into tangible form. Mastering this body involves aligning the physical, emotional, mental, and spiritual aspects of the self to create a harmonious, high-frequency state of being.

Through the Cosmic Flame, a universal source of divine energy, the activation and continuous expansion of the light body become accessible, grounding the Starseed's journey of ascension in both the spiritual and physical realms.

The Light Body as a Vessel for Higher Consciousness

The light body is a multidimensional field of energy that allows the soul to operate beyond the constraints of the physical body and lower-dimensional limitations. It is through this body that Starseeds can access the wisdom of higher realms, communicate with cosmic guides, and engage with the cosmic grid of light that surrounds Earth. The light body vibrates at a frequency beyond the dense energies of the 3D world, and as it develops, it opens gateways to experiences of the 4D and 5D realms, ultimately leading to full ascension into higher planes of consciousness.

Mastering the light body means continuously evolving this energetic structure to accommodate the soul's ever-increasing connection to the divine. At its core, the light body is not static; it is an ever-expanding and dynamic energy field that responds to the thoughts, emotions, and spiritual practices of the individual. As Starseeds progress on their path, the light body becomes the primary vessel through which their higher self interacts with the world, making it crucial to its mastery for the soul's ascension journey.

One of the key challenges in light body mastery is the balancing of higher frequencies with the demands of physical life. The physical body, rooted in 3D reality, often struggles to integrate the intense, high-frequency light of the upper dimensions. This dissonance can manifest as physical discomfort, emotional upheaval, or spiritual confusion. Therefore, the work of mastering the light body involves not just expanding into higher frequencies but grounding these energies in a way that creates harmony between all levels of being.

Advanced Techniques for Light Body Expansion

The expansion of the light body requires sustained spiritual practice and a deep commitment to growth and transformation. While the initial stages of light body activation often focus on clearing blockages and raising one's vibrational frequency, mastery involves cultivating a state of continual openness to the divine and the Cosmic Flame's transformative power. There are several key techniques that can help facilitate the expansion and mastery of the light body:

Advanced Meditation Practices

Meditation remains one of the most powerful tools for light body mastery. However, as one advances on their path, meditative practices must evolve to meet the demands of higher consciousness. In the advanced stages, meditation becomes less about quieting the mind and more about expanding the self into the vastness of the cosmos. During these practices, Starseeds are encouraged to visualize their light body expanding, enveloping their physical form, and extending outwards to connect with the cosmic grid of light.

A key aspect of advanced meditation is the invocation of the Cosmic Flame. Through focused intention, you can call upon the Cosmic Flame to infuse your light body with divine energy, accelerating its growth and deepening your connection to the higher dimensions. The Cosmic Flame serves as a purifier and activator, ensuring that any lingering lower-vibrational energies are transmuted and replaced with the pure frequencies of love, light, and cosmic wisdom.

Daily Integration of Light Frequencies
Mastering the light body involves integrating higher-dimensional light into every aspect of daily life. This can be achieved through mindfulness, where you consciously maintain a high vibrational state even during mundane tasks. Starseeds are encouraged to develop a practice of continuously grounding light frequencies into their being. This could involve frequent energy check-ins throughout the day, visualizing the Cosmic Flame surrounding and supporting the light body, and allowing this energy to permeate through all levels of your being—physical, emotional, and mental.

A critical part of this practice is learning to hold light in challenging situations. The more you can maintain your vibrational frequency during moments of stress, conflict, or emotional difficulty, the more mastery you gain over your light body. By anchoring the higher frequencies of your light body in moments of difficulty, you train yourself to remain aligned with your higher self and the divine, regardless of external circumstances.

Sacred Movement and Breathwork

While meditation and visualization are essential for light body expansion, movement and breathwork also play a crucial role in integrating higher frequencies into the physical body. Practices such as yoga, tai chi, and qi gong can help facilitate the flow of energy throughout the body, ensuring that the light frequencies are distributed evenly and harmoniously. Breathwork, in particular, can be used to activate the energy centers within the body, allowing the Cosmic Flame to flow through these channels and expand the light body.

The breath serves as a bridge between the physical and spiritual realms, and conscious breathing practices can help raise your vibration, clear energetic blockages, and expand the light body. Starseeds are encouraged to engage in breathwork that incorporates the intention of drawing in cosmic light with each inhalation and releasing any lower vibrations with each exhalation. As the light body becomes more active, this process becomes a natural way of maintaining its frequency and supporting its continued growth.

Maintaining the Light Body in the Physical Realm

One of the greatest challenges for Starseeds who have activated and expanded their light body is maintaining this high-frequency state while remaining grounded in the physical world. The Earth's dense energy can often feel heavy and limiting to those who have expanded their consciousness into higher realms, making it essential to develop practices that allow you to remain grounded while still connected to the higher dimensions.

Grounding techniques are critical for maintaining the balance between your light body and your physical existence. Walking barefoot on the Earth, spending time in nature, and connecting with the natural elements can help anchor the light body in a way that supports its expansion. Additionally, maintaining a healthy and balanced lifestyle, including proper nutrition, hydration, and rest, is essential for supporting the physical body as it adapts to the increasing frequencies of the light body.

Another key aspect of maintaining the light body is emotional and mental clarity. As you expand your light body, it is important to release any emotional or mental patterns that no longer serve your highest good. The Cosmic Flame can assist in this process by transmuting old emotional energies and thought forms, allowing you to align more fully with your higher self and the divine.

The Role of the Cosmic Flame in Light Body Mastery

The Cosmic Flame continues to be a guiding force throughout the process of light body mastery. Its energy not only supports the initial activation of the light body but also serves as a continual source of purification, expansion, and alignment. By working with the Cosmic Flame, you can ensure that your light body remains in harmony with the divine plan, free from lower vibrational energies and fully aligned with your soul's purpose.

In its advanced stages, the Cosmic Flame becomes more than just a tool for transformation—it becomes a companion in your journey toward ascension. Starseeds who have mastered their light body often describe a deep, intimate connection with this divine energy, experiencing it as a source of unconditional love, wisdom, and guidance. By maintaining a conscious relationship with the Cosmic Flame, you can continue to evolve your light body and deepen your connection to the higher realms.

Ascension Through Light Body Mastery

Mastering the light body is not the end of the journey but rather a gateway to even greater levels of spiritual evolution. As the light body becomes more active and aligned with the divine, Starseeds gain access to new levels of consciousness, spiritual gifts, and multidimensional experiences. These gifts can be used not only for personal growth but also for assisting others on their own ascension journeys and contributing to the collective evolution of humanity.

Ultimately, light body mastery is about embodying the fullness of your divine nature here on Earth. It is about becoming a living expression of the higher realms, bringing the light of the cosmos into the physical world, and anchoring it for the benefit of all beings. As you continue to work with the Cosmic Flame and expand your light body, you align more fully with your soul's highest purpose and move ever closer to the realization of full ascension.

In mastering the light body, you step into your role as a bridge between worlds, a beacon of light for others, and a vessel for the divine to work through. The journey of ascension is an ongoing process of growth, evolution, and transformation, and mastering the light body is one of the most significant steps along this path. With the Cosmic Flame as your guide, the light body becomes not only a vehicle for ascension but also a source of profound spiritual empowerment, leading you ever closer to the ultimate realization of your soul's highest potential.

COLLECTIVE STARSEED ASCENSION

The Role of Starseeds in Earth's Evolution

Every era of human existence has been marked by subtle yet profound shifts in consciousness, driven by forces that transcend the boundaries of our physical world. In this current epoch of spiritual awakening, Starseeds stand at the forefront of Earth's evolution, not merely as passive observers but as active participants in a cosmic transformation. Their presence on Earth is no coincidence; it is part of a carefully orchestrated plan designed to guide humanity through one of the most critical phases of its evolutionary journey.

Starseeds, with their heightened awareness and deep-rooted connection to higher dimensions, are not separate from the collective fabric of humanity. Rather, they are interwoven into it, serving as catalysts for spiritual change. Their purpose goes beyond personal ascension; they carry a collective mission to assist Earth in its ascension and to raise the consciousness of all beings inhabiting the planet.

The Earth's Ascension Process and the Starseed Mission

The concept of Earth's ascension is tied to the planet's shift from a predominantly 3D consciousness, which is rooted in physicality, separation, and duality, to a higher-dimensional state that embraces unity, love, and oneness. This process is not solely a physical transformation but also an energetic and spiritual evolution. Earth itself, as a living, conscious being, is on its own ascension path, moving toward higher frequencies and shedding the dense energies of fear, division, and materialism that have characterized much of human history.

At the heart of this planetary ascension process is the awakening of human consciousness. For millennia, human beings have been caught in cycles of karmic patterns and limiting beliefs that have kept them disconnected from their divine essence. As Earth moves toward higher dimensions, humanity is being called to release these old patterns and align with the higher frequencies of love, compassion, and interconnectedness. This shift, however, is not happening passively; it requires active participation from those who have already begun to embody these higher states of consciousness.

This is where Starseeds play an integral role. Starseeds, with their cosmic origins and inherent connection to higher realms, are naturally attuned to the energies of ascension. They come to Earth with the intention of assisting in the collective awakening, helping others to remember their divine nature and guiding humanity through the challenges and opportunities of this evolutionary shift. The presence of Starseeds on Earth at this time is no accident—it is part of a cosmic plan to elevate the consciousness of the planet and ensure that humanity transitions smoothly into the new era of enlightenment.

Starseeds as Anchors of Light

One of the primary roles of Starseeds in Earth's evolution is to serve as anchors of light. Through their spiritual practices, meditations, and conscious actions, Starseeds help to ground the higher-dimensional energies of love, light, and divine wisdom into the physical plane. This process is essential for stabilizing the planetary grid of light, a complex energetic matrix that supports the ascension of Earth and its inhabitants.

As anchors of light, Starseeds have the ability to hold high frequencies in their energy fields, which can then be shared with others. Their presence alone can have a profound impact on the energy of their surroundings, subtly influencing those around them to begin their own awakening process. Starseeds often find themselves in positions where they act as beacons of hope, guidance, and healing for others, whether consciously or unconsciously.

In anchoring these energies, Starseeds also play a critical role in balancing the collective energy of humanity. During times of turmoil, fear, or collective upheaval, the light held by Starseeds serves as a counterbalance to the denser energies that may arise. Their ability to remain aligned with higher frequencies, even in the face of adversity, helps to stabilize the collective field and prevent humanity from falling back into old patterns of fear and separation.

The Activation of Earth's Light Grid

Beyond their individual roles, Starseeds are also part of a larger collective effort to activate Earth's planetary light grid. This grid is a vast, interconnected network of energy lines, often referred to as ley lines, that crisscross the planet, forming a geometric matrix of light. These energy lines are not just physical in nature but also energetic, carrying the frequencies of higher dimensions and serving as conduits for divine energy.

The activation of this light grid is crucial for Earth's ascension, as it allows for the free flow of higher-dimensional energies throughout the planet. When the grid is fully activated and aligned with higher frequencies, it acts as a support system for both the planet and humanity, enabling smoother transitions into higher states of consciousness. Starseeds, with their unique energetic signatures, are often drawn to key points along this grid, where their presence can help to activate or strengthen these energy lines.

Many Starseeds feel a deep calling to travel to certain sacred sites on Earth, such as Stonehenge, the Pyramids of Giza, or Mount Shasta. These locations are often powerful energy vortexes that are directly connected to the planetary grid. Through their meditations, rituals, and intentional work at these sites, Starseeds help to activate and maintain the flow of higher-dimensional energies into the planet. This work is not always done consciously; often, Starseeds are simply drawn to these locations without fully understanding why, only to later realize the significant energetic work they have been a part of.

The Challenges of the Starseed Mission

While the role of Starseeds in Earth's evolution is undoubtedly profound, it is not without its challenges. Many Starseeds experience a sense of isolation or disconnection upon incarnating on Earth, as they often feel out of place in a world that operates on a lower vibrational frequency than what they are accustomed to. The density of Earth's energy, coupled with the collective amnesia that occurs upon incarnation, can make it difficult for Starseeds to remember their true origins and mission.

Furthermore, the process of holding and anchoring higher frequencies in a world that is still largely governed by fear, division, and materialism can be taxing. Starseeds may find themselves facing resistance, both internally and externally, as they work to bring about the necessary changes for Earth's ascension. This resistance can manifest in many forms, from personal challenges to societal obstacles, and it requires a great deal of inner strength and resilience to stay the course.

However, these challenges are not insurmountable. In fact, they are a crucial part of the Starseed mission, as they provide opportunities for growth, healing, and the deepening of one's spiritual practice. By overcoming these challenges, Starseeds not only advance their own personal ascension but also contribute to the collective evolution of humanity. The Cosmic Flame, which serves as a source of divine support and guidance, is always available to assist Starseeds in navigating these challenges and staying aligned with their mission.

The Ripple Effect of Starseed Ascension

The work of Starseeds, while often subtle, has a ripple effect that extends far beyond their immediate surroundings. As more Starseeds awaken to their mission and begin actively participating in Earth's ascension, their collective efforts create waves of change that influence the entire planet. Each Starseed who steps into their role as a beacon of light contributes to the overall elevation of human consciousness, making it easier for others to awaken and begin their own spiritual journeys.

This ripple effect is not limited to Earth alone. Starseeds are part of a much larger cosmic network, and their work on Earth has far-reaching implications for the greater universe. As Earth ascends, it creates a vibrational shift that resonates throughout the cosmos, influencing other planets, dimensions, and beings. The ascension of Earth is part of a much larger cosmic plan, and Starseeds are key players in ensuring that this plan unfolds as intended.

Embracing the Role of the Cosmic Leader

As Starseeds awaken to their role in Earth's evolution, they are also being called to step into positions of leadership. This leadership is not about control or authority but rather about embodying the qualities of love, compassion, and wisdom that are necessary for guiding humanity through the ascension process. Starseeds are being asked to lead by example, to be living embodiments of the higher frequencies that they have come to anchor on Earth.

The journey of a Starseed is not always easy, but it is deeply rewarding. By embracing their role in Earth's ascension, Starseeds have the opportunity to not only advance their own spiritual evolution but also to contribute to the collective awakening of humanity. The time for this work is now, and as more Starseeds step into their power, the path toward a new Earth becomes clearer and more attainable for all. With the support of the Cosmic Flame and the guidance of higher-dimensional beings, Starseeds are well-equipped to lead humanity through this pivotal moment in its evolutionary journey, creating a world that is aligned with the divine principles of love, unity, and ascension.

Awakening the Global Grid of Light

The energy that surrounds Earth is vast, intricate, and connected to both the physical and spiritual dimensions. For Starseeds, understanding and participating in the awakening of the global grid of light is one of the most profound contributions they can offer to the collective ascension of Earth. This grid, also referred to as the planetary light grid or ley lines, forms an interconnected network that stretches across the globe, acting as a conduit for higher-dimensional energies and cosmic wisdom to flow into Earth. It is a system as old as the planet itself, designed to support Earth's energetic balance, spiritual evolution, and the ascension process.

In ancient times, civilizations such as the Egyptians, Mayans, and Druids built their sacred temples, pyramids, and monuments along these ley lines. These sites were not only places of worship but also energetic hubs where cosmic energies could be anchored and distributed. Today, as Earth approaches a new stage in its evolutionary journey, Starseeds are being called to reawaken these ancient energy systems and activate the global grid of light.

The Nature of the Global Grid of Light

The global grid of light is an energetic matrix that overlays the physical structure of Earth. It is often described as a web of interconnected energy lines that form a geometric pattern, linking sacred sites, power spots, and vortexes around the planet. These energy lines, known as ley lines, carry high-frequency energies that resonate with the divine blueprint of Earth. They are conduits for the flow of life force energy, or chi, that sustains the planet's vitality and supports the spiritual growth of all beings.

The grid is not limited to the physical Earth; it extends into the higher dimensions, connecting Earth to the cosmic realms and the greater universe. It serves as a bridge between the physical and spiritual planes, allowing the exchange of information, light codes, and frequencies from higher dimensions to reach Earth. This connection is essential for the planet's ascension, as it enables Earth to receive the necessary energies to raise its vibrational frequency and evolve into a higher state of being.

For millennia, the global grid has been in a state of dormancy or partial activation. While some sacred sites and ley lines have remained active, much of the grid has been disrupted by the dense energies of fear, division, and materialism that have dominated human consciousness. The awakening of the grid is a process of restoring the flow of high-frequency energies and reactivating the sacred connections that support Earth's ascension.

The Role of Starseeds in Awakening the Grid

Starseeds play a critical role in the awakening of the global grid of light. Their inherent connection to higher dimensions, along with their ability to hold and anchor high-frequency energies, makes them uniquely suited for this work. Many Starseeds feel a deep calling to visit sacred sites, participate in global meditations, or engage in energy work focused on reactivating the grid. Whether they are consciously aware of it or not, Starseeds are often drawn to places where their energetic presence is needed to support the reawakening of the grid.

One of the most important ways Starseeds can assist in this process is through their ability to act as conduits for higher-dimensional energies. By engaging in practices such as meditation, energy healing, and intentional rituals, Starseeds can channel cosmic energies into the grid, helping to clear any blockages and restore the flow of light. This work is often done in collaboration with the Earth itself, as well as with higher-dimensional beings such as galactic guides and ascended masters, who oversee the planetary ascension process.

The reawakening of the grid is not just about restoring ancient energy lines; it is also about creating new pathways for higher-dimensional energies to flow. As humanity continues to evolve, new grids of light are being activated that align with the higher frequencies of the ascended Earth. Starseeds are instrumental in anchoring these new grids, helping to establish a foundation for the next phase of planetary evolution.

Activating the Grid Through Sacred Sites

Throughout the world, there are sacred sites and energy

vortexes that are key points on the global grid of light. These locations, often marked by ancient temples, pyramids, stone circles, and other monuments, serve as anchors for cosmic energy. They are places where the veil between the physical and spiritual realms is thin, allowing for a direct connection to higher dimensions. Activating these sacred sites is a crucial part of reawakening the global grid.

Many Starseeds feel an inner calling to visit these sites, either physically or energetically. By meditating at these locations, performing rituals, or simply being present with an open heart, Starseeds can help to reactivate the energy lines that flow through these places. In some cases, Starseeds may be guided to perform specific ceremonies or energy work that aligns with the unique frequency of the site, further supporting the activation process.

It is important to recognize that the activation of the grid is not limited to physical travel. Starseeds can also connect with sacred sites remotely through meditation and intention. By tuning into the frequency of a particular location, Starseeds can send energy and light to support the awakening of the grid, no matter where they are in the world. This practice of remote grid activation is especially important as more and more Starseeds begin to work together on a global scale.

The Collective Awakening and the Grid

The awakening of the global grid of light is intimately connected to the collective awakening of humanity. As more individuals begin to raise their consciousness and align with higher frequencies, the grid becomes more active and powerful. Conversely, as the grid becomes more activated, it supports the awakening of greater numbers of people, creating a feedback loop that accelerates the ascension process.

Starseeds, through their work with the grid, help to amplify this collective awakening. By anchoring higher-dimensional energies into the grid, they make it easier for others to access these frequencies and begin their own spiritual journeys. The more the grid is activated, the more it supports humanity's transition into a new era of consciousness, where love, unity, and oneness are the guiding principles.

This collective awakening is not limited to humanity alone. The activation of the grid also supports the ascension of the planet itself, as well as all of the beings who inhabit it, including animals, plants, and the elemental forces of nature. The global grid of light is a living system that supports the evolution of all life on Earth, and its reawakening is a crucial step in the planet's journey toward ascension.

Challenges and Opportunities in Awakening the Grid

The work of awakening the global grid of light is not without its challenges. The dense energies of fear, division, and materialism that have dominated the planet for so long can create resistance to the flow of higher-dimensional energies. Starseeds may encounter obstacles in their work, both on a personal and collective level. These challenges may manifest as energetic blockages, physical fatigue, or even emotional resistance to the process of awakening.

However, these challenges also present opportunities for growth and healing. By working through these obstacles, Starseeds can deepen their connection to the Earth and the cosmic realms, further strengthening their ability to anchor light. Each challenge that is overcome serves as a stepping stone toward greater mastery and alignment with the higher frequencies of the ascended Earth.

It is also important for Starseeds to remember that they are not alone in this work. The reawakening of the grid is a collective effort, supported by countless Starseeds, lightworkers, and higher-dimensional beings around the world. By coming together in unity and collaboration, Starseeds can amplify their efforts and create a powerful wave of light that supports the awakening of the global grid.

A New Earth Awaits

The awakening of the global grid of light is one of the most important steps in the ascension of Earth. As the grid becomes more active, it supports the planet's transition into higher dimensions, creating a foundation for the New Earth—a reality rooted in love, unity, and divine consciousness. Starseeds are at the forefront of this transformation, playing a vital role in reawakening the grid and anchoring the energies of ascension.

Through their dedication to this work, Starseeds are helping to create a world where the divine blueprint of Earth can unfold in its highest potential. The activation of the grid is not just about the physical Earth; it is about the awakening of the collective soul of humanity and the creation of a new reality that reflects the highest frequencies of love and light.

As Starseeds continue to awaken the global grid, they are contributing to the creation of a new era for Earth—one where humanity can live in harmony with the planet and the cosmos. This is the vision of the New Earth, and it is within reach for all who are willing to step into their roles as co-creators of this divine transformation.

Using the Cosmic Flame for Global Healing

The world is undergoing a profound transformation. As the energies of ascension continue to amplify, the need for healing —both on a personal and planetary level—becomes increasingly urgent. The Cosmic Flame, a divine force of transformation and purification, offers an unparalleled tool for addressing the wounds of the Earth and its inhabitants. Starseeds, with their innate connection to higher realms and cosmic energies, are uniquely positioned to channel the power of the Cosmic Flame for global healing.

Healing the planet is not just an abstract notion; it is an intimate and necessary part of the collective ascension process. The dense energies of fear, division, and exploitation that have accumulated on Earth over millennia need to be transmuted if the planet and humanity are to rise to a higher state of consciousness.

The Cosmic Flame: A Universal Healing Force

The Cosmic Flame is a universal energy of transformation. It embodies the essence of divine alchemy, capable of burning away lower vibrations and transmuting them into higher frequencies of love, harmony, and unity. This energy exists beyond the limitations of time and space, making it an ideal force for healing on a planetary scale. The Flame can be directed toward specific areas in need of healing—whether it be geographical regions, ecosystems, or collective human consciousness.

For millennia, mystics, shamans, and spiritual healers have tapped into similar universal energies through prayer, ritual, and meditation. However, Starseeds, with their unique alignment to cosmic energies and their mission to aid in Earth's ascension, have an even deeper connection to the Cosmic Flame.

It is not only a tool but a core aspect of their spiritual identity and purpose.

When invoked consciously, the Cosmic Flame acts as a purifying fire that can cleanse and heal the deepest wounds of the planet. This flame works in harmony with the higher forces of the universe, aligning its power with divine will. In doing so, it catalyzes profound shifts in the vibrational state of the planet, elevating the consciousness of all life on Earth.

The Role of Starseeds in Planetary Healing

Starseeds are born with a deep inner knowing that they are here for a purpose beyond the material world. Part of this purpose is their role in assisting with the healing of the planet. Starseeds carry within them an inherent ability to channel energies from the higher dimensions, acting as conduits for the Cosmic Flame to flow into the Earth's energetic grid.

This process is not about saving the Earth, but about participating in a co-creative relationship with the planet. Gaia, the consciousness of Earth, is a living, sentient being who is fully engaged in her own ascension. However, the collective density created by humanity's lower vibrations has made it difficult for Gaia to fully release these energies on her own. Starseeds, through their conscious work with the Cosmic Flame, can help Gaia transmute these energies and raise the planet's frequency.

Planetary healing requires focus, intention, and a deep sense of responsibility. Starseeds must first do the inner work of clearing their own energetic blocks and aligning with higher frequencies before they can effectively channel healing energies for the Earth. As they heal themselves, they become clearer vessels for the Cosmic Flame to flow through. The more aligned a Starseed is with their own divine essence, the more powerful their healing work for the planet becomes.

Techniques for Using the Cosmic Flame in Global Healing

There are several techniques that Starseeds can use to invoke the Cosmic Flame for planetary healing. These practices combine meditation, visualization, and intention, allowing Starseeds to direct the transformative energy of the Flame to where it is most needed.

One of the most effective methods involves connecting with the Earth's energetic grid, also known as the global grid of light. This grid is a network of energy lines that crisscross the planet, connecting sacred sites, power vortexes, and other places of high vibrational energy. The Cosmic Flame can be channeled into this grid to cleanse and purify areas that have been impacted by negative energies, such as war, environmental destruction, or collective fear.

To begin this process, Starseeds should enter a deep meditative state and visualize the Earth as a radiant sphere of light. They can then call upon the Cosmic Flame, visualizing it descending from the higher dimensions and flowing into the planet's grid. As the Flame moves through the grid, it purifies and raises the vibrational frequency of the Earth, dissolving any lower energies it encounters.

Another technique involves working directly with specific geographical regions or ecosystems that are in need of healing. For example, Starseeds can focus on areas that have been devastated by natural disasters, pollution, or conflict. By invoking the Cosmic Flame and directing it toward these regions, Starseeds can help to transmute the dense energies that are contributing to the imbalance. This process not only heals the land but also raises the collective consciousness of the people living in those areas.

It is important to note that the healing work should be done with the highest respect for Gaia's sovereignty. Starseeds are not here to impose their will upon the Earth, but rather to assist in her natural healing process. By working in harmony with Gaia's energy, Starseeds can ensure that the healing work is aligned with the planet's own ascension path.

Collective Healing and the Cosmic Flame

The power of the Cosmic Flame is amplified when used in collective healing efforts. As more Starseeds join together in focused intention, the energy of the Flame becomes exponentially more powerful. Group meditations, global healing events, and collective rituals all serve to magnify the healing energy being directed toward the planet.

In recent years, there has been a surge of global meditations and collective efforts to heal the Earth. These gatherings of like-minded souls create a powerful vortex of energy that can be directed toward the healing of specific regions or the entire planet. Starseeds who participate in these collective efforts are contributing to a larger wave of healing that is sweeping across the globe.

Working together, Starseeds can also help to anchor new frequencies of light into the Earth's grid. These frequencies are being transmitted from higher dimensions as part of the ascension process, and they are essential for the planet's evolution. By consciously anchoring these frequencies through group meditations or rituals, Starseeds can assist in stabilizing the new energies and supporting the Earth in her transition to a higher state of being.

The Ripple Effect of Planetary Healing

When Starseeds use the Cosmic Flame for planetary healing, the effects are far-reaching. Not only does this work heal the Earth, but it also has a profound impact on the collective consciousness of humanity. As the dense energies that have held humanity in a state of fear and separation are transmuted, people begin to awaken to their true nature as beings of light.

The ripple effect of planetary healing can be seen in the rise of global movements focused on environmental sustainability, social justice, and spiritual awakening. As the Earth heals, humanity is inspired to create a world that is more aligned with the principles of unity, love, and harmony. The Cosmic Flame, through its transformative power, plays a key role in this process.

Starseeds, through their dedication to planetary healing, are helping to pave the way for a new Earth—one that is in alignment with the higher frequencies of the cosmos. Their work is not only a service to the planet but also a service to all of humanity and future generations.

Embracing the Role of Planetary Healers

As we move deeper into the ascension process, the need for planetary healing will only increase. Starseeds are being called to step into their roles as healers, not only for themselves but for the Earth and all its inhabitants. This is a sacred responsibility, one that requires dedication, focus, and a deep connection to the divine.

Through the use of the Cosmic Flame, Starseeds have the power to heal on a global scale. By working with this divine energy, they can help to transmute the dense energies that have kept the Earth in a lower vibrational state and support the planet's transition into a new era of light and love.

The journey of planetary healing is ongoing, and each step taken by a Starseed brings us closer to the realization of a world in harmony with the cosmos. As you embrace your role as a planetary healer, know that your work is part of a greater divine plan, one that is unfolding with every breath, every intention, and every act of love.

Leading the Collective Ascension Effort

As the Starseed awakening accelerates, the collective ascension of humanity and the Earth becomes a central focus for those who have answered the call of their higher purpose. Starseeds are not only here to experience their individual spiritual evolution but to serve as guides, catalysts, and leaders for the greater shift in consciousness. This leadership role is essential in navigating the challenges of global transformation, helping humanity to transition from a lower vibrational state into one that reflects unity, love, and higher wisdom.

Leading the collective ascension effort requires a deep understanding of the cosmic energies at play, an unwavering connection to the Cosmic Flame, and a profound commitment to the evolution of both the Earth and its inhabitants.

The Call to Cosmic Leadership

For Starseeds, the call to leadership in the collective ascension effort often begins with a quiet but undeniable inner knowing. This sense of purpose may first manifest as a desire to help others, to alleviate suffering, or to inspire deeper spiritual growth within communities. Over time, it becomes clear that this purpose extends far beyond individual acts of service; it is about contributing to the global awakening on a planetary scale.

Cosmic leadership is not about personal power or recognition. Rather, it is a humble and sacred duty that requires a willingness to act as a bridge between the higher realms and the material world. Starseeds who step into leadership are tasked with holding a steady frequency of love and light amidst the chaos of transformation, guiding others with clarity, compassion, and courage. They must embody the teachings of the Cosmic Flame, becoming living examples of its power to transmute lower energies into higher states of being.

In the collective ascension effort, leadership can take many forms. Some Starseeds may find themselves drawn to teaching or facilitating spiritual groups, while others may focus on healing work, environmental activism, or creating new systems that reflect higher consciousness. Whatever form this leadership takes, it is always rooted in the intention to serve the highest good of all beings and to support the Earth's ascension process.

Holding Space for Collective Healing

One of the primary roles of an ascension leader is to hold space for collective healing. As the Earth and humanity move through the ascension process, deep wounds—both personal and planetary—will come to the surface to be healed. These wounds, which have been accumulated over millennia, include trauma from war, environmental destruction, social injustice, and the suppression of spiritual knowledge.

For healing to occur on a collective level, there must be individuals who are capable of holding space for the intensity of these energies without being overwhelmed or drawn into fear. Starseed leaders are uniquely equipped for this task. Through their connection to the Cosmic Flame, they are able to remain anchored in higher frequencies, allowing them to transmute dense energies and guide others through the healing process.

Holding space involves more than simply being present; it requires deep empathy, active listening, and the ability to create environments where others feel safe to release old patterns and embrace new possibilities. Whether through group meditations, healing circles, or one-on-one interactions, Starseed leaders create a container for transformation, allowing the collective to move through its healing journey with grace and support.

This space-holding extends beyond the immediate people in a Starseed leader's circle. On a metaphysical level, these leaders are also working with the Earth's energetic grid, anchoring the higher frequencies of the Cosmic Flame into the planet's energy systems. This work helps to stabilize the collective ascension process, making it easier for humanity to integrate the incoming waves of cosmic light and higher-dimensional energies.

Advanced Techniques for Leading Ascension Efforts

Leading the collective ascension effort involves more than just spiritual knowledge; it requires the application of advanced techniques that can assist in guiding humanity through the complex transitions of this time. These techniques, rooted in the principles of energy work, meditation, and cosmic alignment, help Starseed leaders to maintain their own energetic integrity while facilitating the evolution of the collective.

One such technique is the use of group meditations that focus on anchoring the Cosmic Flame into specific areas of the Earth or the collective consciousness. In these meditations, Starseeds gather with the intention of invoking the Cosmic Flame and directing its energy toward planetary healing, the dissolution of lower-vibrational thought forms, or the activation of higher-dimensional frequencies. These group efforts create powerful energetic vortices that can assist in accelerating the ascension process for both individuals and the planet.

Another advanced technique involves working with sacred geometries and energy grids. Starseed leaders who are proficient in this area can use sacred symbols, such as the Flower of Life or the Merkabah, to create energetic templates that hold the frequencies of ascension. These templates can be anchored into the Earth's grid, where they serve as stabilizing forces for the incoming cosmic energies. This work is especially important during times of planetary upheaval or cosmic events, such as eclipses, solstices, or other astrological alignments that bring heightened energy to the planet.

Additionally, Starseed leaders may use sound healing, light language, and other vibrational tools to assist in the collective ascension. These modalities work by aligning the frequencies of the human body and the Earth with the higher-dimensional energies of the ascension process. When used in group settings, these tools can create powerful resonance fields that uplift the entire collective, making it easier for people to release lower energies and embrace their own ascension path.

Leading with Compassion and Clarity

As the world undergoes profound shifts, it is natural for fear and uncertainty to arise within the collective. People may feel disoriented by the rapid changes taking place, or they may resist the ascension process out of fear of the unknown. In these moments, Starseed leaders must remain anchored in their higher awareness, offering compassion, clarity, and reassurance to those who are struggling.

Compassion is a key element of leadership during the ascension process. It allows leaders to meet people where they are, without judgment or expectation, and to guide them with gentleness and understanding. At the same time, Starseed leaders must also maintain clarity in their vision of what is possible. By holding a clear vision of the new Earth—one based on unity, love, and higher consciousness—leaders can help others to see beyond the challenges of the present moment and to embrace the opportunities for growth and transformation.

In times of crisis, Starseed leaders are called to act as beacons of light, reminding others of their own divine nature and the greater purpose of the ascension process. This requires emotional resilience and a deep trust in the unfolding of the divine plan. By staying connected to the Cosmic Flame and aligning with the higher realms, Starseed leaders can offer guidance that is both practical and spiritually grounded, helping humanity to navigate the ascension with grace.

Preparing for the New Earth

As the collective ascension continues, the vision of the new Earth becomes more tangible. This new reality, rooted in higher-dimensional consciousness, will be characterized by harmony, cooperation, and a deep connection to the cosmos. Starseed leaders play a vital role in preparing for this new Earth by guiding humanity through the final stages of the ascension process and helping to anchor the frequencies that will support this higher state of being.

Preparing for the new Earth requires a long-term perspective. While the ascension process is already underway, it is a gradual transformation that will unfold over years, if not decades. Starseed leaders must therefore remain patient and committed, knowing that their work is contributing to a larger divine plan. This preparation involves not only spiritual guidance but also practical efforts to create new systems, structures, and communities that reflect the values of the new Earth.

These communities, often referred to as "light communities" or "conscious collectives," will serve as models for the rest of humanity. In these spaces, people will live in alignment with the principles of love, unity, and respect for all life. Starseed leaders are at the forefront of these efforts, creating environments where the higher frequencies of the new Earth can be fully embodied and experienced.

Embracing the Role of Cosmic Leadership

Stepping into the role of a leader within the collective ascension effort is both an honor and a responsibility. Starseed leaders are here to serve as way-showers, guiding humanity through the most profound transformation it has ever experienced. This role requires dedication, humility, and a deep connection to the Cosmic Flame, as well as the courage to face the challenges of the ascension process with grace.

As you embrace your role as a leader in the ascension effort, know that you are not alone. You are part of a vast network of Starseeds, lightworkers, and cosmic beings who are all working toward the same goal: the evolution of the Earth and humanity into a higher state of consciousness. By leading with love, compassion, and clarity, you are helping to create a new reality —one that reflects the divine light of the cosmos and the infinite potential of the human spirit.

EMOTIONAL ALCHEMY AND SOUL HEALING

The Emotional Impact of Awakening

The path of spiritual awakening is deeply transformative, yet the emotions it stirs can be overwhelming. For Starseeds, this journey often begins with a powerful, almost inexplicable yearning—a sense that they are meant for something greater, that their purpose transcends the mundane. As this call grows louder, it sparks the initial steps toward awakening. But with this spiritual awakening comes an array of emotional challenges, as Starseeds begin to shed old identities and patterns while stepping into their higher selves.

The emotional impact of awakening is profound. Feelings of isolation, confusion, and fear may surface as the familiar world shifts and the Starseed's inner reality expands. Relationships, careers, and even long-held beliefs about the nature of reality can be called into question, creating a sense of destabilization.

The Initial Shock of Awakening

For many Starseeds, the first stage of awakening can feel like an earthquake within the soul. As the veils between the spiritual and physical worlds begin to thin, their perception of reality alters, often suddenly. This can manifest as an intense spiritual epiphany, a moment of profound clarity, or an overwhelming sense of connection to the cosmos. But equally, it can bring disorientation, as the Starseed grapples with feelings of being "different" or "other."

The emotional shock of awakening can be likened to the feeling of being unmoored, drifting in a vast ocean with no clear direction. Old ways of thinking, behaving, and interacting no longer resonate, yet the path forward is not immediately clear. This can create a deep sense of grief as Starseeds mourn the loss of their former selves and the reality they once knew. Simultaneously, excitement for the new and unknown rises, often in a conflicting dance with fear of change.

This period of awakening requires great compassion and patience, both from the Starseed themselves and from those around them. Self-care is critical during this stage, as the emotional body processes these shifts. It is essential for Starseeds to acknowledge their feelings without judgment, allowing space for the full range of emotions to be expressed and released.

The Challenge of Isolation and Loneliness

One of the most common emotional challenges Starseeds face during their awakening is a profound sense of isolation. As they begin to attune to higher frequencies, their worldview and energetic field shift dramatically. Friends, family, and even partners may not understand the spiritual transformation that is taking place, leading to feelings of separation and loneliness.

Starseeds often feel like they do not belong in the world around them. They may feel disconnected from societal norms, finding that conventional goals, such as career advancement or material success, no longer hold meaning. This can create an emotional rift between the Starseed and their external environment, as they long for deeper connections based on shared spiritual values.

Loneliness during the awakening process is a natural consequence of spiritual evolution, as the soul moves through a period of recalibration. However, it is crucial for Starseeds to recognize that this feeling of isolation is temporary. As they continue their journey, they will attract like-minded souls—other Starseeds, lightworkers, and spiritual seekers—who are on similar paths. These soul connections will provide the support, understanding, and companionship needed to ease the pain of loneliness.

It is also important for Starseeds to seek out spiritual communities or groups where they can share their experiences and receive validation for their journey. Whether through meditation circles, online communities, or personal mentorship, connecting with others who understand the awakening process can help alleviate feelings of isolation and offer valuable emotional support.

Anxiety and Uncertainty in the Face of Change

The process of awakening often brings about dramatic changes, not only within the self but also in external circumstances. Jobs may fall away, relationships may end, and long-held goals may be abandoned as the Starseed begins to align with their soul's true purpose. While these changes are necessary for growth, they can also trigger anxiety, fear, and a sense of loss.

Anxiety during awakening is often rooted in the unknown. As old structures dissolve, there may be a period of uncertainty where the future feels unclear. Starseeds may wonder what their new path will look like, how they will support themselves, or how they will navigate relationships that no longer resonate. This uncertainty can create a sense of inner tension, as the ego struggles to maintain control in the face of transformation.

To ease this anxiety, it is essential for Starseeds to cultivate trust in the divine unfolding of their journey. The process of awakening is guided by higher forces, and while the path may not always be clear, it is leading toward greater alignment with the soul's true purpose. Meditation, grounding practices, and energy work can help Starseeds release fear and anxiety, bringing them back into a state of calm and inner peace.

Surrendering to the process of change is a key aspect of emotional alchemy during awakening. Rather than resisting the shifts that are occurring, Starseeds are encouraged to embrace them with an open heart. This requires faith in the cosmic plan and an understanding that every ending is a new beginning, leading them closer to their authentic selves.

Navigating Emotional Waves: From Despair to Joy

Awakening is often described as a journey of extremes, where the Starseed swings between moments of intense despair and profound joy. This emotional rollercoaster can be disorienting, as one day may bring feelings of elation, connection, and spiritual clarity, while the next day may be marked by sadness, frustration, or a sense of being lost.

These emotional waves are a natural part of the spiritual journey, as the soul clears out old energy patterns, karmic imprints, and limiting beliefs. When despair arises, it is often a sign that deep healing is taking place. The old must be purged to make way for the new, and this process can bring to the surface emotions that have long been suppressed.

At the same time, moments of joy and spiritual connection serve as glimpses of the new reality that is emerging. During these moments, Starseeds may experience heightened states of consciousness, feelings of oneness with the universe, and a deep sense of purpose. These experiences provide reassurance that they are on the right path, even when the road feels uncertain.

To navigate these emotional waves, Starseeds are encouraged to practice emotional alchemy. This involves recognizing emotions as energy in motion and allowing them to flow without attachment or resistance. Rather than identifying with feelings of despair or joy, Starseeds can observe them as temporary states that are part of the greater process of transformation. By remaining present with their emotions and practicing self-compassion, Starseeds can move through these waves with grace.

The Role of Emotional Healing in Ascension

The emotional impact of awakening is not just a byproduct of the ascension process; it is an essential part of it. As Starseeds awaken to higher consciousness, they must heal the emotional wounds that have been carried throughout lifetimes. These wounds may include feelings of abandonment, rejection, unworthiness, or fear, all of which must be transmuted in order to fully embody the soul's higher light.

Emotional healing is an act of self-love. It requires the Starseed to face their shadow, to acknowledge the parts of themselves that have been hidden or denied, and to bring these aspects into the light of consciousness. This process can be painful, as it involves revisiting past traumas and releasing deeply ingrained emotional patterns. However, it is through this healing that the Starseed is able to rise into their true power.

The Cosmic Flame is a powerful tool for emotional healing. By invoking this sacred energy, Starseeds can transmute lower emotional frequencies, such as fear or grief, into higher states of love and compassion. The Cosmic Flame acts as a purifier, burning away the emotional blockages that prevent the soul from ascending to its highest potential.

Through this process of emotional alchemy, Starseeds learn to master their emotions rather than be controlled by them. They develop emotional resilience, allowing them to navigate the challenges of awakening with greater ease. As they heal their own emotional wounds, they also contribute to the healing of the collective consciousness, helping to raise the vibration of humanity as a whole.

Embracing Emotional Alchemy on the Ascension Journey

The emotional impact of awakening is a profound part of the Starseed's ascension journey. It challenges the soul to release old identities, heal deep-seated wounds, and embrace a new way of being. While this process can be emotionally intense, it is also an opportunity for profound growth, transformation, and spiritual empowerment.

As Starseeds move through the emotional waves of awakening, they are reminded that they are not alone. They are supported by the Cosmic Flame, by their higher selves, and by the collective energy of other Starseeds who are also walking this path. Together, they are co-creating a new reality—one that is built on the foundation of love, unity, and emotional mastery.

By embracing emotional alchemy, Starseeds can move through the challenges of awakening with grace and compassion, knowing that every emotion is part of the greater process of soul evolution. As they heal and transmute their own emotions, they become beacons of light for others, guiding humanity toward a future of higher consciousness and collective ascension.

Healing Past-Life Wounds Through

the Cosmic Flame

The process of spiritual awakening for Starseeds is not limited to the here and now. It is deeply interwoven with the soul's experiences across lifetimes, dimensions, and realities. Starseeds, in particular, carry within them not only the lessons and growth of this life but also the karmic imprints, unresolved energies, and emotional wounds from past lives. These echoes from the soul's journey often manifest as blocks, limiting beliefs, or deep-seated fears that hinder spiritual evolution. Healing these past-life wounds is essential for Starseeds to move forward on their ascension path, and the Cosmic Flame offers a profound means of doing so.

The Cosmic Flame, as a universal force of transformation, has the power to transmute the heavy, dense energies that accompany past-life traumas. Through its purifying fire, Starseeds can access these ancient memories, clear the karmic imprints left behind, and heal the emotional and energetic wounds that still influence their present lives.

Recognizing Past-Life Wounds in the Present

One of the first steps in healing past-life wounds is recognizing how they manifest in the current lifetime. Often, past-life traumas are hidden beneath the surface of conscious awareness but can influence thoughts, behaviors, and emotional reactions. These unresolved energies may show up as irrational fears, chronic emotional pain, or patterns of self-sabotage that seem disconnected from present experiences. For example, a Starseed may harbor a deep fear of abandonment or betrayal that has no basis in their current life but is tied to a significant event in a previous incarnation.

Past-life wounds can also manifest in physical symptoms or chronic health issues that resist conventional healing methods. These physical manifestations are the body's way of holding onto unresolved energies from previous lives. Through intuitive awareness, meditation, and working with the Cosmic Flame, Starseeds can begin to uncover the deeper roots of these patterns and symptoms.

Dreams and spontaneous flashbacks are another common way past-life memories surface. Starseeds may have vivid dreams of different lifetimes, landscapes, or cultures, often accompanied by strong emotional responses. These dreams are not merely products of the subconscious mind but are windows into the soul's journey across time and space. By paying attention to these dreams and meditating on their meaning, Starseeds can begin to piece together the story of their soul's evolution and identify the wounds that need healing.

The Karmic Imprints of Past Lives

At the core of many past-life wounds are karmic imprints—energetic patterns or lessons that the soul carries from one lifetime to the next. Karma, as a universal law, is not about punishment but about balance and growth. Each soul has a unique karmic blueprint, which outlines the lessons it must learn and the energies it must clear to achieve full ascension.

Some past-life wounds are the result of unresolved karma. For instance, a Starseed may have experienced a traumatic event in a past life—such as betrayal, violence, or loss—that left an energetic imprint on their soul. If this karma was not fully resolved in that lifetime, the soul carries it into subsequent incarnations, where it continues to influence the Starseed's experiences and emotional landscape.

Healing these karmic imprints requires understanding the lessons they hold. Often, past-life wounds present themselves as repeated patterns in relationships, career, or health, as the soul seeks to balance the energies it has accumulated over lifetimes. By bringing these patterns into conscious awareness, Starseeds can begin to work with the Cosmic Flame to clear the karmic residue and transmute it into higher frequencies of love, compassion, and forgiveness.

The Power of the Cosmic Flame in Healing Past Lives

The Cosmic Flame is a potent tool for healing past-life wounds because of its transformative and purifying qualities. When invoked with intention, the Cosmic Flame acts as a bridge between the conscious mind and the deeper layers of the soul's memory. It has the ability to penetrate the layers of density created by unresolved trauma, allowing Starseeds to access the karmic imprints and emotional energies stored in their energetic field.

To begin the healing process, Starseeds are encouraged to enter into a meditative state and connect with the Cosmic Flame. This sacred fire can be visualized as a brilliant, radiant light that flows through the body, dissolving blockages and purifying the energetic pathways. With each breath, the Starseed can invite the Cosmic Flame to illuminate the memories and wounds from past lives that are ready to be healed.

As the past-life memories surface, it is essential for the Starseed to approach them with compassion and non-judgment. The healing process is not about reliving past traumas but about acknowledging their presence, understanding their lessons, and releasing them from the energetic body. The Cosmic Flame assists in this by transmuting the dense, stagnant energies associated with the wound into higher frequencies of light and love. As this transmutation occurs, the Starseed may experience a profound sense of release, as the emotional and energetic weight of the past is lifted.

The Cosmic Flame also supports forgiveness, both of self and others. Many past-life wounds are tied to relationships or events where forgiveness was not given or received. By working with the Cosmic Flame, Starseeds can release the emotional charge of these past experiences, allowing forgiveness to flow and freeing the soul from karmic entanglement.

Soul Retrieval and Reclaiming Lost Fragments

In addition to clearing karmic imprints, healing past-life wounds often involves a process of soul retrieval. Over the course of many lifetimes, the soul may become fragmented as a result of trauma, loss, or fear. These fragments are parts of the self that become disconnected from the whole in order to protect the soul from pain. However, these lost fragments carry essential aspects of the Starseed's wisdom, power, and purpose, and their return is necessary for full healing.

Soul retrieval is a sacred practice that allows the Starseed to reclaim these lost fragments and reintegrate them into their being. The Cosmic Flame can be used to guide this process, creating a safe and supportive space for the soul fragments to return. By inviting the lost parts of the self back into the light of the Cosmic Flame, the Starseed can heal the fractures within their soul and restore their wholeness.

The process of soul retrieval is often accompanied by feelings of empowerment and clarity, as the Starseed reconnects with their innate gifts and strengths that have been hidden or dormant. It is a profound act of self-love and acceptance, allowing the Starseed to step more fully into their true essence and purpose.

Moving Forward with Grace and Wisdom

As past-life wounds are healed through the Cosmic Flame, Starseeds experience a profound shift in their energy and consciousness. The clearing of karmic imprints, the release of emotional blockages, and the reintegration of lost soul fragments all contribute to a greater sense of wholeness and alignment with the soul's higher purpose.

Moving forward, Starseeds are encouraged to continue working with the Cosmic Flame as a tool for ongoing healing and transformation. While the healing of past lives may bring immediate relief and clarity, it is also an ongoing process. The soul's journey through ascension is one of continuous growth, and as new layers of consciousness are revealed, there may be more aspects of the past that require healing.

The grace and wisdom gained through healing past-life wounds become invaluable assets on the path to ascension. With each wound that is healed, the Starseed becomes more aligned with their higher self, more attuned to their soul's mission, and more capable of contributing to the collective ascension of humanity and Earth.

Ultimately, healing past-life wounds through the Cosmic Flame is an act of liberation. It frees the Starseed from the burdens of the past, allowing them to step fully into the present with clarity, strength, and purpose. As they heal themselves, they also contribute to the healing of the collective, anchoring higher frequencies of light and love on the planet. Through this process, Starseeds fulfill their cosmic purpose, guiding humanity toward a brighter, more unified future.

Navigating Dark Nights of the Soul

The journey of spiritual ascension is not always marked by blissful enlightenment or serene insights. For many Starseeds, the most transformative phases of growth come through what is often called the "dark night of the soul." This period of deep spiritual crisis can feel overwhelming, characterized by feelings of isolation, despair, confusion, and a disconnection from one's higher purpose. Yet, it is in these moments of profound darkness that the seeds of light are planted. The dark night is not an end but a passage—a sacred initiation on the path to greater spiritual evolution.

The Dark Night as a Catalyst for Transformation

The dark night of the soul can be triggered by many factors. For some, it arises after a major life event, such as the loss of a loved one, the end of a relationship, or a significant shift in career or identity. For others, the dark night occurs spontaneously, as a sudden and inexplicable sense of spiritual disorientation or emotional collapse. At its core, the dark night is a profound stripping away of the ego and the illusions of separation, leading to a confrontation with the deeper truths of the soul.

This process can be extremely challenging for Starseeds, who are often sensitive to the energies of both the Earth and the cosmos. The dark night can evoke feelings of abandonment, as if the divine has withdrawn its presence, leaving the soul to navigate the abyss alone. Yet, this perceived abandonment is part of the greater plan for spiritual transformation. In truth, the dark night is an invitation to let go of old identities, beliefs, and attachments that no longer serve the soul's highest purpose. It is a purging, a death of the false self, so that the true self—the divine essence within—can emerge more fully.

The Cosmic Flame as a Beacon of Light in the Darkness

During the dark night of the soul, Starseeds may feel as though they have lost their connection to the cosmic energies that once guided them. The Cosmic Flame, however, remains ever-present, even when it seems distant or dim. It is during this time that the Cosmic Flame becomes a crucial ally in the process of healing and rebirth. As a purifying force, the Cosmic Flame can help Starseeds to burn away the illusions and fears that surface during the dark night, allowing them to reconnect with their inner light and higher purpose.

To work with the Cosmic Flame during the dark night, Starseeds must first acknowledge and accept the emotions and experiences that arise. This is not a time to push away or deny the pain, but rather to sit with it, observe it, and allow it to be transmuted by the fire of the Cosmic Flame. Through meditation, visualization, and focused intention, Starseeds can invite the Cosmic Flame to enter their hearts and minds, burning away the layers of fear, doubt, and confusion that cloud their vision.

In this sacred process, the Cosmic Flame serves not only as a source of healing but also as a beacon of hope. It reminds Starseeds that even in the darkest of nights, the light of the soul remains unbroken. The flame burns within, guiding the soul through the shadows and illuminating the path forward. By trusting in the Cosmic Flame and surrendering to its transformative power, Starseeds can emerge from the dark night stronger, clearer, and more aligned with their divine purpose.

Embracing Surrender and Trust in the Process

One of the most difficult aspects of navigating the dark night of the soul is the need for surrender. The dark night is a journey into the unknown, where the old ways of understanding and controlling one's reality no longer apply. For Starseeds, who are often highly intuitive and spiritually aware, this loss of control can feel disorienting and frightening. The natural impulse may be to resist the darkness, to try to "fix" the situation or force a return to the light. However, the dark night cannot be bypassed or rushed. It requires patience, trust, and a willingness to surrender to the process.

Surrender in this context does not mean giving up or becoming passive. Rather, it is an active choice to trust in the wisdom of the soul and the divine plan. It is a recognition that the dark night is a necessary part of the ascension journey, designed to clear away the egoic attachments that prevent the soul from fully embodying its higher self. By surrendering to the Cosmic Flame and allowing its purifying fire to work within, Starseeds open themselves to the deeper healing that can only occur through this process.

Trust is also essential during this time. While the dark night may feel endless, it is not. It is a temporary phase, one that serves a greater purpose in the soul's evolution. Trusting in the divine timing of the process allows Starseeds to move through the darkness with grace, knowing that the light will return. The Cosmic Flame, as a symbol of divine presence, offers reassurance that even in the depths of despair, the soul is being held, guided, and protected.

Rebirth and Renewal After the Dark Night

The conclusion of the dark night of the soul is often marked by a profound sense of rebirth. Like a phoenix rising from the ashes, the soul emerges from the darkness transformed, carrying with it new wisdom, clarity, and strength. The illusions of the ego have been burned away, leaving behind a deeper connection to the true self—the aspect of the soul that is eternal, divine, and connected to the cosmic flow of the universe.

For Starseeds, this rebirth is a powerful moment of realization. The dark night, though painful, has served as a catalyst for greater spiritual alignment and purpose. The lessons learned during this time are invaluable, as they reveal the deeper truths of the soul's journey and its role in the collective ascension of humanity and the Earth.

In the aftermath of the dark night, Starseeds may find themselves more attuned to the energies of the Cosmic Flame, as well as to their own inner flame. The connection to the divine is strengthened, and the path forward becomes clearer. The darkness, once feared, is now seen as a necessary part of the cycle of growth and evolution. It is through this understanding that Starseeds can move forward with greater confidence, knowing that they are not only capable of navigating the challenges of the spiritual path but also of using those challenges as opportunities for profound transformation.

Integrating the Lessons of the Dark Night

As Starseeds emerge from the dark night of the soul, it is important to take time for reflection and integration. The insights gained during this time are deeply personal and transformative, and they require space to fully settle into the consciousness. Journaling, meditating, and continuing to work with the Cosmic Flame can help Starseeds to integrate the lessons of the dark night and apply them to their daily lives.

The dark night is also an invitation to deepen one's spiritual practice. As the ego's grip is loosened, the soul becomes more open to the guidance of the divine. This is an ideal time to strengthen the connection to the Cosmic Flame through regular meditation, prayer, and energy work. By continuing to nurture this connection, Starseeds can maintain the clarity and alignment gained through the dark night and use it as a foundation for further spiritual growth.

In addition, the dark night often awakens a greater sense of empathy and compassion, both for oneself and for others. Having walked through the depths of the soul's shadows, Starseeds are now more equipped to support others who may be going through similar experiences. The wisdom gained from the dark night can be shared with the broader collective, helping to guide others through their own spiritual challenges and into the light of ascension.

The Gift of the Dark Night

Though the dark night of the soul is often feared for its intensity and challenges, it is ultimately a gift. It is a sacred rite of passage that strips away the illusions of the ego and reveals the true essence of the soul. For Starseeds, the dark night is a profound opportunity to align more deeply with their cosmic purpose and to step into their role as healers, guides, and lightbearers for the Earth.

By working with the Cosmic Flame during this time, Starseeds can navigate the darkness with grace, healing the wounds of the past and emerging into the light with greater clarity, strength, and purpose. The dark night is not the end of the journey—it is the doorway to a new beginning, one that leads to higher levels of consciousness, spiritual empowerment, and collective ascension.

Advanced Emotional Alchemy for Full Healing

The ascension journey for Starseeds is an intricate process of transformation, where each phase requires the soul to rise beyond its current limitations, expanding into greater states of awareness and embodiment. One of the most profound aspects of this journey is the need for emotional healing—a process that goes far beyond the mere resolution of everyday emotional conflicts. Advanced emotional alchemy is a vital practice for Starseeds aiming to fully heal deep-seated wounds, transmute past traumas, and release energetic blocks that may hinder their ascension.

The Nature of Emotional Alchemy

At its core, emotional alchemy refers to the process of transforming raw emotional energy into higher frequencies of love, compassion, and wisdom. For Starseeds, emotions are not simply fleeting sensations but powerful energetic forces that shape the flow of spiritual energy throughout the body and mind. Emotions such as fear, anger, grief, and shame can create blockages in the energetic field, preventing the free flow of higher vibrational energies that are essential for ascension.

Advanced emotional alchemy requires a deep understanding of the nature of emotions and their role in spiritual evolution. Rather than seeing emotions as something to be avoided or suppressed, emotional alchemy invites Starseeds to embrace these feelings fully, recognizing them as gateways to higher states of consciousness. The Cosmic Flame, as a tool of purification and transmutation, plays a key role in this process, offering a divine force that helps dissolve negative emotional imprints and replace them with higher frequencies of light and love.

Working with the Cosmic Flame for Emotional Healing

The Cosmic Flame serves as a transformative energy that burns away the lower vibrational residues of unresolved emotional experiences. In advanced emotional alchemy, Starseeds are called to use the Cosmic Flame in a focused and intentional way, inviting its healing power into their emotional bodies.

To begin this process, Starseeds must first become fully present with their emotional states. This requires a willingness to confront emotions that may have been buried or suppressed for years or even lifetimes. Techniques such as deep meditation, breathwork, and journaling can help bring these emotions to the surface. Once the emotions are acknowledged, the next step is to consciously invite the Cosmic Flame to transmute these energies.

The visualization of the Cosmic Flame entering the heart center is a powerful practice for emotional transmutation. As the Flame enters, it begins to dissolve the emotional blocks that are held within the heart, allowing the energy of love and compassion to flow freely. Starseeds may also feel a physical release as the energetic weight of unresolved emotions is lifted, replaced by a profound sense of peace and inner clarity.

As the Cosmic Flame burns through these emotional layers, it is essential for Starseeds to remain open and receptive to the process. Emotional alchemy can be an intense experience, as deep feelings of sorrow, anger, or fear rise to the surface. However, it is important to trust that the Cosmic Flame is doing its work, transforming these emotions into the fuel for ascension. In time, this process leads to a more purified emotional body, one that is capable of holding higher frequencies of light.

Healing Ancestral and Past-Life Emotional Wounds

For many Starseeds, the emotional wounds that need healing are not solely from their current lifetime. Often, these wounds are carried forward from past lives, encoded in the soul's memory and passed down through ancestral lines. These karmic imprints can manifest as recurring patterns of emotional pain, unhealthy relationship dynamics, or deep-seated fears that seem difficult to explain.

In advanced emotional alchemy, it is crucial to recognize and address these ancestral and past-life wounds. The Cosmic Flame is uniquely equipped to facilitate this type of healing, as its divine energy transcends time and space, reaching into the very core of the soul's past experiences.

One method for healing ancestral and past-life wounds is through past-life regression meditations, where Starseeds can journey back to previous incarnations and identify the emotional imprints that are still affecting them today. During these meditations, the Cosmic Flame can be invoked to cleanse and heal the emotional body, releasing any residual karmic energy that no longer serves the soul's highest good.

Another powerful technique is working with the Cosmic Flame

to heal ancestral lines. This involves sending the energy of the Flame back through the generations, healing the emotional traumas that have been passed down from ancestors. This process not only frees the Starseed from these inherited emotional blocks but also brings healing to the entire family line, creating a ripple effect of transformation that extends beyond the individual soul.

Releasing Fear and Embracing Love

One of the most significant aspects of advanced emotional alchemy is the transmutation of fear. Fear is one of the most pervasive and limiting emotions that can prevent Starseeds from fully embracing their divine potential. Whether it manifests as fear of failure, fear of rejection, or fear of the unknown, this emotion can create powerful energetic blockages that hinder spiritual growth.

To overcome fear, Starseeds must first acknowledge it without judgment. Fear often arises when the ego feels threatened or when the soul is about to make a significant leap in consciousness. Rather than resisting or denying fear, advanced emotional alchemy calls for Starseeds to bring the Cosmic Flame into the heart of this emotion, allowing it to transmute fear into love.

This process begins with acceptance. Starseeds are encouraged to sit with their fear, understanding its origins and the lessons it holds. As the Cosmic Flame is called upon to burn through the fear, the energy of love begins to replace it. Love is the highest frequency in the universe, and when fear is transformed into love, the soul is able to rise to new levels of awareness and connection with the divine.

The practice of embracing love as the dominant emotional frequency is an ongoing process. As Starseeds continue to work with the Cosmic Flame, they learn to recognize fear as a temporary state, one that can be transmuted through the power of love. Over time, this shift in emotional energy leads to greater spiritual liberation and alignment with the soul's higher purpose.

Integrating Emotional Alchemy into Daily Life

Emotional alchemy is not a one-time event but an ongoing practice that Starseeds can integrate into their daily lives. As emotions arise in response to life's challenges, Starseeds can use the Cosmic Flame to continuously transmute these energies, maintaining a state of emotional balance and harmony.

One way to integrate emotional alchemy into daily life is through regular meditation and energy work. By setting aside time each day to connect with the Cosmic Flame, Starseeds can clear any emotional blockages that have built up throughout the day, ensuring that their energy field remains open and receptive to higher frequencies.

Another important practice is cultivating mindfulness and self-awareness. By becoming more conscious of their emotional responses, Starseeds can identify when they are holding onto lower vibrational emotions and immediately begin the process of transmutation. This level of emotional mastery allows Starseeds to move through life with greater ease and grace, knowing that they have the tools to heal and transform any emotional challenge that arises.

As Starseeds continue to practice emotional alchemy, they will notice a profound shift in their overall emotional state. The lower vibrational emotions of fear, anger, and grief will become less dominant, while the higher frequencies of love, joy, and compassion will begin to take their place. This transformation not only enhances personal well-being but also contributes to the collective ascension of humanity and the Earth.

The Power of Emotional Alchemy in Ascension

Advanced emotional alchemy is one of the most transformative practices for Starseeds on the path of ascension. By working with the Cosmic Flame to transmute lower vibrational emotions into higher frequencies, Starseeds can achieve profound healing, both on a personal and ancestral level. This process allows the soul to release the burdens of the past, clear emotional blockages, and embrace the higher frequencies of love and compassion.

As Starseeds master the art of emotional alchemy, they become more aligned with their divine purpose and better equipped to navigate the challenges of the ascension journey. The emotional body, once weighed down by fear and pain, becomes a vessel for the free flow of cosmic energy, empowering Starseeds to embody their highest potential and contribute to the collective healing of the planet. The Cosmic Flame, as a tool of divine transformation, will continue to serve as a guiding light on this sacred journey, offering its purifying power to those who seek full emotional healing and ascension.

SACRED COSMIC RELATIONSHIPS

Recognizing Soulmates and Twin Flames in the Ascension Journey

In the sacred path of spiritual evolution, the relationships we form are not merely coincidental. As Starseeds, we are connected to a greater cosmic web, interwoven with souls who play vital roles in our ascension. Two of the most powerful and transformative connections we experience during our spiritual journey are those with soulmates and twin flames. Recognizing and understanding these relationships is crucial for Starseeds as they navigate the profound transitions of ascension.

Soulmates and twin flames are not just romantic labels; they are spiritual connections that serve unique and essential purposes. As Starseeds evolve, these relationships emerge to catalyze growth, healing, and transformation. The deep emotional and energetic bonds with soulmates and twin flames act as mirrors, reflecting back the parts of ourselves that require healing, love, and alignment with the higher self.

The journey of ascension becomes deeply enriched through the relationships with soulmates and twin flames, but it is also often fraught with emotional intensity and spiritual challenges. These relationships stretch beyond the confines of this lifetime and carry energies from multiple lifetimes and dimensions. As such, recognizing these connections in the context of the ascension journey opens the door to powerful transformations that support the evolution of the soul.

Soulmates: Catalysts for Growth

The term "soulmate" is often misunderstood as purely romantic, but in truth, soulmates can appear in many forms, such as friends, family members, or even significant mentors. Soulmates are souls that share a deep, preordained connection with us, and they cross our paths in this lifetime to help us learn vital lessons and catalyze spiritual growth. They are, in essence, mirrors that reflect both the light and the shadow aspects of our being, revealing the areas where we need to heal and evolve.

For Starseeds, soulmates play a crucial role in triggering awakenings and breakthroughs. These relationships may not always be easy or harmonious, but they are always purposeful. Soulmates often help Starseeds confront unresolved emotional patterns, karmic imprints, and wounds from both this life and past incarnations. Through these relationships, the soul is offered an opportunity for deep healing and expansion.

Recognizing a soulmate connection is often accompanied by a sense of familiarity, as though the soul recognizes the other on an intrinsic level. There is a magnetic pull, and interactions with a soulmate often carry a profound emotional resonance, even in non-romantic contexts. The spiritual contract between soulmates is designed to accelerate the Starseed's ascension process, and while some soulmate relationships last a lifetime, others may be fleeting yet transformative encounters.

The intensity of soulmate relationships can sometimes lead to emotional turbulence, as unresolved issues are brought to the surface for healing. However, it is important to remember that these challenges are part of the soul's evolutionary process. The Cosmic Flame, as a tool for transmutation, can be used to heal any wounds or emotional blockages that arise within these connections. By invoking the Cosmic Flame, Starseeds can purify the energies of these relationships, ensuring that they serve their highest purpose in the ascension journey.

Twin Flames: The Divine Mirror

While soulmates play a significant role in spiritual growth, the connection with a twin flame is a relationship of an entirely different magnitude. A twin flame is often described as the other half of the soul, split into two separate incarnations. Unlike soulmates, who may be numerous, there is only one twin flame. The reunion with a twin flame is one of the most profound experiences a Starseed can have on the path of ascension, as it represents the ultimate merging of the self with the divine.

The twin flame relationship is marked by an intense, almost electric energy. Meeting a twin flame often feels like encountering a perfect reflection of oneself. This reflection, however, is not just of the light aspects of the self, but also of the shadow. In this way, twin flames serve as a powerful mirror, revealing both the highest potential and the deepest wounds within each other. The purpose of this connection is to accelerate the process of healing and spiritual evolution by forcing both individuals to confront and integrate all aspects of themselves.

One of the key characteristics of a twin flame connection is its ability to push both individuals toward their highest potential. The reunion with a twin flame often triggers a rapid acceleration of spiritual growth, as the connection amplifies the energy and consciousness of both souls. Twin flames are not necessarily romantic partners, although the intensity of the connection can often lead to romantic or deeply emotional involvement. The core purpose of this relationship, however, transcends romance—it is about spiritual union and the collective ascension of both individuals.

Twin flame relationships are often challenging because they demand complete emotional transparency and the release of ego-based fears. The twin flame serves as a catalyst for deep transformation, but this process can be overwhelming. It is common for twin flames to go through periods of separation, as both individuals may need time and space to process the intense energies and heal before they can fully reunite. During these periods, the Cosmic Flame can be invoked to assist in the transmutation of any emotional or energetic imbalances, helping both souls to align with their highest selves.

Ultimately, the twin flame reunion is about the integration of the masculine and feminine energies within both individuals. It is a journey toward wholeness and divine union, not just with each other, but with the universal consciousness. As twin flames work through their individual challenges, they come closer to embodying their divine purpose and aligning with the higher frequencies necessary for ascension.

Recognizing the Signs of Soulmate and Twin Flame Connections

Recognizing a soulmate or twin flame connection often begins with an undeniable sense of familiarity and a deep emotional resonance. For many Starseeds, meeting a soulmate or twin flame feels like "coming home." There is an unspoken understanding and an energetic connection that transcends time and space. These relationships often feel destined, and the synchronicities surrounding their arrival in one's life are too significant to be dismissed as mere coincidence.

However, the path of recognizing and navigating these relationships can be fraught with challenges. The intensity of the connection may bring up unresolved fears, insecurities, and emotional wounds that have been buried for years, or even lifetimes. For Starseeds, it is essential to approach these relationships with an open heart and a willingness to embrace the lessons they offer. The Cosmic Flame serves as a vital tool in this process, helping to purify and transmute any negative energies or emotional blocks that arise.

In recognizing a twin flame, Starseeds may experience what is known as "twin flame telepathy," where both individuals can sense each other's emotions and thoughts, even when separated by great distances. This psychic connection is one of the hallmarks of the twin flame relationship, as it reflects the deep soul bond between the two individuals. This connection often feels divine and purposeful, as though the universe itself has conspired to bring the two souls together for a higher mission.

Soulmates, on the other hand, may not always trigger the same level of psychic connection, but their role in the Starseed's life is equally important. Soulmates often arrive during times of great change or transition, offering support, guidance, and the opportunity for healing. While these relationships may not always be as intense as twin flame connections, they are vital for the Starseed's spiritual journey and offer valuable lessons in love, compassion, and forgiveness.

Embracing the Cosmic Purpose of These Connections

The recognition of soulmates and twin flames is not just about identifying these relationships but understanding their greater purpose in the context of ascension. Both soulmates and twin flames serve as catalysts for spiritual growth, helping Starseeds to heal, evolve, and align with their divine purpose. These connections are not meant to be idealized or romanticized but rather embraced as sacred opportunities for transformation.

As Starseeds continue on their ascension journey, it is essential to view these relationships through the lens of cosmic purpose. Whether it is a soulmate who offers a temporary but powerful lesson, or a twin flame whose presence catalyzes profound inner transformation, these connections are all part of the soul's greater plan for evolution. By working with the Cosmic Flame, Starseeds can purify and heal the emotional and energetic aspects of these relationships, ensuring that they serve the highest good of both individuals involved.

Ultimately, the recognition of soulmates and twin flames is about embracing the divine connections that support the soul's ascension. These relationships, whether brief or lifelong, serve as spiritual mirrors, reflecting back the truth of who we are and guiding us toward greater alignment with our higher selves. By honoring the sacred purpose of these connections and working with the Cosmic Flame for healing and transformation, Starseeds can fully embrace the love, wisdom, and growth that these relationships offer on the path of ascension.

Healing and Balancing Cosmic Relationships

The relationships Starseeds encounter on their ascension journey are imbued with deeper spiritual purpose. Whether with soulmates, twin flames, or kindred spirits, each connection offers an opportunity to grow, heal, and expand. Yet, like all transformative experiences, these relationships come with challenges—emotional wounds from past lives, karmic imprints, and the complexities of balancing energies that are often more cosmic than personal. Healing and balancing these relationships becomes a necessary part of the Starseed's spiritual evolution, for only through harmony can one align with the cosmic forces that guide the ascension path.

As Starseeds become more attuned to the cosmic frequencies that fuel their awakening, they often discover that their most intimate relationships reflect this spiritual growth. The deep emotional ties formed in these connections serve as both mirrors and magnifying glasses, bringing to light unresolved issues and energetic imbalances. Healing and balancing these relationships is an essential aspect of aligning with the higher vibrations required for ascension.

At the heart of this healing process lies the Cosmic Flame, a tool that Starseeds can use to transmute and clear negative energies, helping to harmonize and strengthen the bonds between themselves and their cosmic partners. The Cosmic Flame, with its transformative and purifying power, offers an avenue for addressing the karmic patterns, emotional wounds, and energetic blocks that often arise in these relationships. Through it, Starseeds can release what no longer serves their highest good, allowing for the relationship to evolve into one of spiritual harmony and growth.

Understanding the Energetic Dynamics of Cosmic Relationships

Cosmic relationships, particularly those involving soulmates and twin flames, are often characterized by their intense energy. These connections go beyond the surface level of interaction, tapping into a deeper energetic and spiritual resonance. For many Starseeds, this intensity can be overwhelming, as the relationship serves to bring to the surface unresolved traumas, insecurities, and fears from this life and past incarnations. The deep soul recognition between Starseeds and their cosmic partners often triggers what is known as "shadow work," wherein both individuals are called to confront the darker aspects of themselves that they have repressed or ignored.

The energies exchanged in these relationships are not just emotional but also energetic. Starseeds, with their heightened sensitivity to cosmic frequencies, can often feel the energetic pull and push of their relationships more acutely than others. This is particularly true for twin flame connections, where the shared soul energy creates an almost magnetic bond that can be both uplifting and challenging. Healing and balancing these energies requires a deep understanding of the spiritual dynamics at play, as well as a commitment to mutual growth and transformation.

Healing cosmic relationships begins with the recognition that these connections are not accidental. They are divinely orchestrated encounters designed to help both individuals ascend to higher states of consciousness. However, this process is not without its difficulties. The intensity of these relationships often brings up old wounds—some from this lifetime, others from past incarnations—that must be healed in order for the relationship to thrive. The Cosmic Flame can be invoked to assist in this healing process, offering a way to transmute the negative energies that arise and replace them with love, harmony, and understanding.

Healing Past-Life Wounds in Cosmic Relationships

One of the most profound aspects of cosmic relationships is their connection to past lives. Many of the relationships Starseeds form, particularly with soulmates and twin flames, are rooted in karmic patterns that have been carried over from previous incarnations. These patterns can manifest as emotional wounds, unresolved conflicts, or a sense of unfinished business between the two individuals. In order to heal and balance these relationships, it is essential to recognize and address these past-life wounds.

Past-life wounds often show up as recurring patterns or themes in the relationship. For example, a Starseed may find themselves repeatedly experiencing feelings of abandonment, betrayal, or unworthiness in their relationships, even when there is no apparent cause in the present. These emotions are often remnants of unresolved issues from previous incarnations, where the soul experienced similar traumas or conflicts. Healing these wounds requires the Starseed to look beyond the surface level of the relationship and explore the deeper karmic ties that bind them to their cosmic partner.

The Cosmic Flame can be used as a powerful tool for healing past-life wounds in relationships. By invoking the Flame, Starseeds can access the higher dimensions of consciousness where these karmic patterns are stored. The Flame's transformative energy helps to dissolve the energetic imprints of past-life traumas, allowing both individuals to move forward in the relationship with a clean slate. This process of healing often leads to a deeper sense of understanding and compassion between the two individuals, as they recognize the shared history that has brought them together in this lifetime.

As these wounds are healed, the relationship begins to evolve into one of greater harmony and balance. The emotional intensity that once characterized the connection gives way to a more peaceful and loving dynamic, where both individuals are free to express their true selves without fear or limitation. This shift is a crucial part of the ascension process, as it allows the Starseed to release the lower vibrational energies associated with past-life traumas and embrace the higher frequencies of love, unity, and spiritual alignment.

Balancing the Masculine and Feminine Energies in Relationships

Another key aspect of healing and balancing cosmic relationships is the integration of the masculine and feminine energies within both individuals. All relationships, whether they are between soulmates, twin flames, or other cosmic partners, involve a dynamic interplay between these two energies. The masculine energy, often associated with action, strength, and logic, complements the feminine energy, which is linked to intuition, nurturing, and emotional depth. In cosmic relationships, achieving a balance between these energies is essential for the relationship to thrive and support both individuals on their ascension journey.

Many of the challenges that arise in cosmic relationships stem from imbalances in these energies. For example, one partner may embody more masculine energy, while the other holds more feminine energy, leading to a dynamic where one individual takes on the role of the provider or protector, while the other assumes the role of the nurturer or emotional guide. While this dynamic can be harmonious, it can also lead to imbalances if one partner feels overwhelmed by their role or if the energies are not equally shared.

The process of balancing the masculine and feminine energies in a relationship requires both individuals to embrace and integrate these energies within themselves. This involves recognizing and honoring the strengths of both the masculine and feminine aspects of the self, as well as working to heal any wounds or imbalances that may exist. The Cosmic Flame can assist in this process by helping to clear any energetic blockages that prevent the full expression of these energies. Through meditation and intention, Starseeds can use the Flame to harmonize the masculine and feminine aspects of their being, creating a more balanced and integrated relationship dynamic.

As the masculine and feminine energies within the relationship become more balanced, both individuals are able to express themselves more authentically and fully. This balance creates a sense of harmony and flow within the relationship, where both partners feel supported and empowered to pursue their individual spiritual paths while also contributing to the collective ascension of the relationship. In this way, the relationship becomes a powerful vehicle for mutual growth, healing, and spiritual evolution.

Embracing the Cosmic Purpose of Relationships

Healing and balancing cosmic relationships is not just about resolving conflicts or addressing emotional wounds—it is about recognizing the higher purpose of these connections. Starseeds are brought together with their soulmates, twin flames, and other cosmic partners for a reason: to support each other on the path of ascension. These relationships serve as catalysts for spiritual growth, offering opportunities for healing, transformation, and the integration of higher frequencies.

By embracing the cosmic purpose of these relationships, Starseeds can move beyond the limitations of the ego and tap into the deeper spiritual significance of their connections. This shift in perspective allows both individuals to approach the relationship with greater compassion, understanding, and love. The challenges that arise in the relationship are no longer seen as obstacles, but as opportunities for growth and healing.

The Cosmic Flame plays a crucial role in this process by helping to purify and transmute the energies of the relationship, allowing both individuals to align with their highest selves. Through meditation, intention, and the invocation of the Flame, Starseeds can release the lower vibrational energies that may be hindering the relationship and create a space of love, harmony, and spiritual alignment.

In cosmic relationships, the journey of healing and balancing is ongoing. As both individuals continue to evolve and ascend, new challenges and opportunities for growth will arise. However, by embracing the cosmic purpose of these relationships and working with the transformative power of the Cosmic Flame, Starseeds can create relationships that are not only harmonious and balanced, but also deeply supportive of their individual and collective ascension journeys.

Using the Cosmic Flame to Strengthen Spiritual Connections

In the grand dance of ascension, where the celestial and the terrestrial intertwine, Starseeds hold the sacred responsibility of nurturing not only their own souls but the spiritual connections they share with others. These connections, formed in the heart of divine purpose, offer profound opportunities for growth, healing, and enlightenment. In cosmic relationships, whether between soulmates, kindred spirits, or twin flames, spiritual connection plays a vital role in each individual's evolution. Using the Cosmic Flame to deepen and strengthen these connections is a powerful practice that enables Starseeds to transcend the limitations of the ego, opening the doorway to true soul communion.

The Cosmic Flame, a potent energetic force that pulses with the frequency of divine love and transformation, offers an unparalleled means of enhancing the spiritual bonds Starseeds share with others. By working with the Cosmic Flame, individuals can align their frequencies with those of their spiritual counterparts, facilitating a flow of energy that is both harmonious and expansive.

The Nature of Spiritual Connections in Cosmic Relationships

Spiritual connections, particularly in the context of Starseeds, are often far more intricate and layered than conventional relationships. These connections transcend the physical realm, often rooted in the soul's past incarnations, the shared mission of ascension, and the higher frequencies of love and unity. Many of these bonds predate the current lifetime, having been forged across numerous lifetimes, dimensions, and cosmic planes. These spiritual relationships are designed to accelerate personal growth, push the boundaries of individual understanding, and support the collective ascension process.

However, with such depth also comes complexity. Spiritual connections can often feel intense, overwhelming, and even disorienting, especially when past-life traumas or karmic imprints surface. In this space, communication between souls often transcends language, moving instead through feelings, energetic exchanges, and telepathic insights. The Cosmic Flame, with its purifying and amplifying power, offers Starseeds the means to clarify and strengthen this communication, allowing both individuals to connect with greater ease, understanding, and resonance.

By invoking the Cosmic Flame in their spiritual practices, Starseeds can remove the energetic blockages that may hinder their connections with others. Whether it is fear, doubt, or unresolved emotional trauma, these blockages often obscure the true nature of the bond, making it difficult for both parties to experience the full depth of their connection. The Cosmic Flame works to transmute these lower energies, replacing them with vibrations of love, clarity, and higher consciousness. In doing so, it opens the pathways for genuine spiritual communion, where both individuals are able to share their soul's light and truth without the interference of ego or past-life wounds.

Deepening Telepathic and Energetic Communication

One of the hallmarks of spiritual connections between Starseeds is the ability to communicate telepathically or energetically. This form of communication bypasses the limitations of language, allowing individuals to share thoughts, emotions, and energy on a soul level. For many Starseeds, this ability is latent, waiting to be fully activated as they ascend through higher states of consciousness. The Cosmic Flame can serve as a catalyst in this process, helping Starseeds tap into their innate ability to communicate telepathically with others.

Telepathic communication, in essence, is the transmission of thoughts, feelings, and information from one mind to another without the use of spoken words. It relies on a deep level of trust and energetic alignment between both individuals. When the Cosmic Flame is invoked, it acts as a conduit for this energetic transmission, clearing away any distortions or interferences that may cloud the message. This allows for a purer, more direct flow of communication that transcends the limitations of physical speech.

Energetic communication, on the other hand, involves the exchange of vibrational frequencies between individuals. This can manifest as a feeling of connection, warmth, or even the sensation of another person's presence, even if they are not physically near. By working with the Cosmic Flame, Starseeds can amplify their ability to send and receive these energetic signals, making it easier to stay connected with their spiritual counterparts across distances and dimensions. The Flame's transformative energy enhances the vibrational resonance between individuals, allowing them to align more fully with each other's frequencies and maintain a deeper connection, regardless of physical proximity.

For those seeking to strengthen these forms of communication, regular meditation with the Cosmic Flame is essential. During meditation, Starseeds can visualize the Flame enveloping both themselves and their spiritual counterpart, creating an energetic bridge that facilitates the flow of thoughts, feelings, and energy. This practice not only deepens the spiritual connection but also fosters a greater sense of unity, trust, and alignment between both parties.

Healing Energetic Imbalances in Spiritual Connections

All relationships, whether spiritual or physical, are subject to energetic imbalances. These imbalances can arise from a variety of sources, including past-life wounds, unresolved emotional traumas, or even the differing vibrational frequencies of the individuals involved. In spiritual connections, particularly those involving soulmates and twin flames, these imbalances can manifest as misunderstandings, emotional distance, or feelings of disconnection.

The Cosmic Flame offers a powerful means of healing these imbalances by working to restore harmony and balance to the energetic field. When invoked, the Flame acts as a purifier, burning away the lower vibrational energies that contribute to these imbalances. It then replaces these energies with frequencies of love, unity, and alignment, allowing the relationship to return to its natural state of harmony.

For Starseeds, healing these imbalances is particularly important, as their relationships often serve as conduits for collective healing and ascension. By restoring balance to their spiritual connections, Starseeds are not only supporting their own growth but also contributing to the greater energetic alignment of the planet. The Cosmic Flame, with its transformative power, enables this healing process by facilitating the transmutation of discordant energies and fostering a deeper sense of connection, unity, and love.

To heal energetic imbalances in their spiritual connections, Starseeds can work with the Cosmic Flame through meditation, intention setting, and energy healing practices. By visualizing the Flame surrounding both themselves and their spiritual counterpart, they can invite its purifying energy to transmute any blockages or imbalances that may be hindering the relationship. This practice helps to realign the vibrational frequencies of both individuals, allowing for a smoother, more harmonious connection.

Strengthening the Spiritual Bond for Collective Ascension

As the ascension process accelerates, spiritual connections between Starseeds play an increasingly important role in the collective awakening of humanity. These connections are not just for personal growth and healing; they are also part of a larger cosmic mission to raise the vibrational frequency of the planet and support the collective ascension process. By strengthening their spiritual bonds, Starseeds can create powerful energetic grids that amplify the ascension energies and contribute to the collective awakening.

The Cosmic Flame is a key tool in this process, as it serves to unify and harmonize the energies of those involved in the spiritual connection. When multiple Starseeds work with the Flame to strengthen their bonds, they create a network of high-frequency energy that can be directed towards the collective good. This network, often referred to as a grid of light, helps to anchor the ascension energies on Earth and facilitates the global shift towards higher consciousness.

For Starseeds seeking to strengthen their spiritual bonds for the purpose of collective ascension, regular group meditations with the Cosmic Flame are highly recommended. These meditations allow individuals to connect their energies, amplifying the vibrational frequency of the group and creating a powerful energetic field that supports both personal and planetary ascension. By working together in this way, Starseeds can contribute to the creation of a new reality—one based on love, unity, and higher consciousness.

As Starseeds continue to ascend, their spiritual connections will only grow stronger, deeper, and more aligned with the divine purpose of collective awakening. Through the use of the Cosmic Flame, these connections can be nurtured, healed, and strengthened, allowing both individuals and the collective to rise into the higher frequencies of love, unity, and spiritual enlightenment. In this way, the Cosmic Flame serves as a bridge, not only between individuals but also between the Earth and the higher realms of consciousness, guiding humanity towards its ultimate destiny of ascension.

Mastering the Sacred Union of Twin Flames for Collective Ascension

The concept of twin flames transcends traditional relationship paradigms, offering a unique lens through which Starseeds can understand the nature of divine love and spiritual partnership. At its core, the twin flame union represents a deep spiritual bond that echoes beyond the constraints of time and space, igniting profound growth, healing, and transformation. When twin flames come together, they do so with a higher purpose: to assist in the collective ascension of humanity by embodying divine love in its purest form.

The journey of twin flames is not always an easy one, as it involves the delicate balance of polarities, the integration of shadow aspects, and the alignment of two souls with a shared cosmic mission. The process requires the mastery of emotional alchemy, forgiveness, and a surrender to the flow of divine timing. Yet, when the union reaches its full potential, the energies of twin flames create a powerful ripple effect, anchoring higher frequencies of love and light that radiate outward to uplift the collective consciousness.

Understanding the Twin Flame Journey

The twin flame journey is a spiritual path that extends far beyond the realm of romantic or emotional connection. It is, at its essence, a union that exists on a soul level—two halves of the same whole, separated at the inception of their existence and destined to reunite for a greater cosmic purpose. Twin flames mirror each other's strengths, weaknesses, and desires, reflecting the full spectrum of their soul's light and shadow. This mirroring often accelerates personal growth and healing, as the twin flame connection brings to the surface all that must be addressed for the individuals involved to ascend into higher states of consciousness.

Unlike traditional relationships, which may center on personal fulfillment or companionship, the twin flame journey is fundamentally about spiritual evolution. Twin flames are called to embody and express unconditional love, not only toward one another but toward the entire planet. This union serves as a microcosm of the ascension process, representing the harmonization of divine masculine and divine feminine energies. Through this sacred balance, twin flames act as energetic anchors for the ascension process, holding space for the collective to transition into higher frequencies of consciousness.

One of the most challenging aspects of the twin flame journey is the process of separation and reunion. Many twin flames experience periods of separation, during which time both individuals are called to do deep inner work, heal past-life wounds, and release karmic imprints. These periods of separation are not punishments, but rather opportunities for growth and preparation for the eventual union. As each individual heals and evolves, they draw closer to their twin flame on an energetic level, aligning their vibrations with the frequency of divine love. It is through this alignment that the reunion becomes possible, allowing the twin flames to step fully into their shared mission.

The Role of the Cosmic Flame in Twin Flame Union

The Cosmic Flame plays a vital role in the twin flame journey, serving as a source of purification, transformation, and energetic amplification. As twin flames work with the Cosmic Flame, they are able to clear the energetic blockages, karmic imprints, and emotional wounds that may hinder their union. The Cosmic Flame assists in dissolving the layers of ego, fear, and doubt that can create separation, allowing both individuals to rise into higher states of awareness and alignment with their divine purpose.

Twin flames are often called to work with the Cosmic Flame during times of intense transformation or challenge. By invoking the Flame, they invite the energies of divine love, clarity, and healing into their connection, transmuting any lower vibrational energies that may be preventing their union. This practice is particularly important during the separation phase, as it helps both individuals to release attachments, heal past wounds, and align with the higher frequencies necessary for their reunion.

In addition to its role in healing and purification, the Cosmic Flame also serves as a bridge between twin flames, strengthening their energetic connection and facilitating telepathic communication. Twin flames often experience a deep sense of connection that transcends physical distance, allowing them to share thoughts, emotions, and energy across time and space. By working with the Cosmic Flame, twin flames can enhance this telepathic connection, allowing for clearer communication and a deeper sense of unity. This connection becomes particularly important as they step into their shared mission, as it allows them to work together seamlessly, even when they are not physically together.

The Cosmic Flame also supports twin flames in the process of emotional alchemy, helping them to transmute the lower vibrational energies that may arise during their journey. As twin flames mirror each other's shadows, it is not uncommon for deep-seated fears, insecurities, and unresolved traumas to come to the surface. The Cosmic Flame assists in transmuting these energies, allowing both individuals to heal and integrate their shadow aspects in a way that fosters growth and union.

The Sacred Union and Collective Ascension

The union of twin flames is not solely for the benefit of the individuals involved; it is a powerful force for planetary and collective ascension. As twin flames come into union, they embody the frequency of divine love, creating a powerful energetic field that radiates outward into the collective consciousness. This energetic field serves as a beacon of light, helping to anchor higher frequencies of love, unity, and harmony on Earth. In this way, twin flames play a vital role in the collective awakening and ascension process.

One of the primary purposes of the twin flame union is to serve as a catalyst for collective healing. The energies of the twin flame connection have the ability to transmute dense, lower vibrational energies on a planetary scale, helping to clear the way for the collective ascension. Through their union, twin flames create a powerful energetic grid that supports the awakening of humanity, facilitating the shift from fear and separation to love and unity. This energetic grid is further strengthened when twin flames work together in service to the collective, using their connection to amplify the ascension energies and support the healing of the planet.

For many twin flames, their shared mission involves working together in some form of spiritual service. This may take the form of leading global meditations, facilitating healing sessions, or guiding others on their ascension journeys. By working together in this way, twin flames are able to magnify their impact, creating a ripple effect that reaches far beyond their immediate surroundings. The energies of the twin flame union are not limited by time or space, allowing twin flames to contribute to the collective ascension process regardless of where they are in the world.

Mastering the Union for Full Ascension

Mastering the sacred union of twin flames requires a deep commitment to personal growth, healing, and spiritual evolution. It is not a journey for the faint of heart, as it involves the continual process of emotional alchemy, shadow work, and surrender to divine timing. However, for those who are willing to do the inner work, the rewards are profound. The twin flame union offers an unparalleled opportunity for growth, healing, and ascension, not only for the individuals involved but for the entire planet.

To master the twin flame union, it is essential to cultivate a deep sense of trust, both in oneself and in the divine plan. Twin flames must learn to trust that their journey is unfolding exactly as it is meant to, even during periods of separation or challenge. This trust allows them to surrender to the process, knowing that their union is guided by a higher purpose.

Working with the Cosmic Flame is also essential in mastering the twin flame union. By regularly invoking the Flame, twin flames can keep their energies aligned with the frequencies of love, unity, and divine purpose. This practice helps to clear away any blockages or distortions that may arise, allowing both individuals to remain in alignment with their highest selves and their shared mission.

As twin flames master their union, they step into their full potential as co-creators of the new Earth. Their union becomes a living expression of divine love, serving as a model for others on the ascension journey. In this way, the twin flame union is not only a personal journey but a collective one, contributing to the awakening and ascension of humanity.

The sacred union of twin flames is a powerful force for personal and planetary ascension. Through their connection, twin flames are able to anchor higher frequencies of love and light on Earth, supporting the collective shift into unity consciousness. By mastering their union and working with the Cosmic Flame, twin flames can fulfill their divine purpose and contribute to the creation of a new reality—one based on love, harmony, and spiritual enlightenment.

GALACTIC WISDOM AND COSMIC GUIDES

Connecting with Galactic Guides and Star Beings

In the expansive cosmos, Starseeds are not alone on their ascension journey. They are accompanied by higher-dimensional beings, known as Galactic Guides, who offer wisdom, protection, and guidance through the transformational process. These cosmic entities operate beyond the physical plane, residing in realms where the vibration is more attuned to the frequencies of love, unity, and divine consciousness. As Starseeds awaken and ascend, connecting with these Galactic Guides becomes an essential component of their spiritual evolution.

For many Starseeds, the call to connect with Galactic Guides begins as a subtle internal pull—a sense of longing or curiosity about the cosmos. This desire often emerges in dreams, meditations, or synchronicities that point toward a broader galactic heritage. Galactic Guides serve as emissaries of light, sent from higher-dimensional realms such as the Pleiades, Sirius, Arcturus, or Andromeda, to assist Earth and her inhabitants during this time of ascension. Each guide carries a unique vibrational frequency, offering specialized knowledge, healing, and support tailored to the needs of the Starseed they are working with.

While the initial stages of connecting with Galactic Guides may seem mysterious or elusive, the process is grounded in the fundamental principle of resonance. Just as Starseeds are drawn to the cosmic fire that ignites their soul's evolution, they are also naturally attuned to the frequencies of the Galactic Guides who are part of their soul family. These guides have been with them throughout multiple lifetimes and across different dimensional experiences, watching over their progress and offering assistance whenever it is needed.

Recognizing the Call of Galactic Guides

The first step in connecting with Galactic Guides is recognizing the signs of their presence. These guides often communicate through subtle means, using symbols, synchronicities, or energetic impressions to draw the attention of the Starseed. For example, recurring patterns such as seeing the same number sequences (like 11:11 or 333), experiencing vivid dreams of otherworldly landscapes, or feeling a deep connection to specific constellations or stars can indicate the presence of a Galactic Guide.

These guides may also send sensations of warmth, tingling, or an overwhelming sense of love during moments of meditation or introspection. Starseeds often report feeling as though they are being enveloped in a loving, protective energy—

this is a hallmark of galactic guidance. Galactic Guides rarely communicate through direct words in the beginning. Instead, they send impressions, images, or feelings that are meant to be decoded intuitively by the Starseed. Over time, as the connection strengthens, this communication may become more explicit, evolving into clearer forms of telepathy or even channeling.

Recognizing the call of Galactic Guides requires sensitivity to one's own inner world. It involves cultivating an awareness of subtle shifts in energy and being open to receiving messages from dimensions beyond the physical. Starseeds who wish to connect with their Galactic Guides are encouraged to establish a regular practice of meditation or quiet reflection. This practice creates the internal space necessary for the subtle frequencies of the guides to be received and understood.

Opening the Channels of Communication

Once a Starseed has become aware of the presence of Galactic Guides, the next step is to open the channels of communication. This process begins by setting a clear intention to connect. Intention is a powerful tool in spiritual work, as it aligns one's energy with the desired outcome. When a Starseed sets the intention to connect with Galactic Guides, they are signaling to the universe—and to the guides themselves—that they are ready to engage in this sacred relationship.

Meditation is one of the most effective methods for establishing this connection. During meditation, the mind becomes quiet, and the vibrational frequency of the individual rises, making it easier to access the higher-dimensional realms where Galactic Guides reside. Starseeds can begin by entering a meditative state, focusing on their breath, and calling upon their guides to make their presence known. It is important to remain patient and open during this process, as the connection may take time to develop. Trusting that the guides are there, even if they are not immediately perceived, is key.

Visualization is another powerful tool for connecting with Galactic Guides. Starseeds can imagine themselves surrounded by a protective light, inviting their guides to step forward and communicate. Some may visualize themselves traveling through the stars, meeting their guides in a sacred space where the connection can take place. Others may prefer to focus on a particular star system or constellation that they feel drawn to, using this as a gateway to their guides.

It is also helpful to keep a journal during this process. Writing down any impressions, thoughts, or feelings that arise during meditation or daily life can provide valuable insight into the messages being transmitted by the guides. Over time, patterns may emerge, and the communication will become clearer. Journaling also helps to build trust in the connection, as it allows the Starseed to reflect on how the guidance they are receiving is manifesting in their life.

Deepening the Relationship with Galactic Guides

As the connection with Galactic Guides grows stronger, the relationship evolves into a deeper, more collaborative partnership. At this stage, the guides may begin to offer more specific guidance related to the Starseed's soul mission, life purpose, or areas of spiritual development. These guides often have a wealth of knowledge to share, ranging from healing modalities to advanced spiritual practices, and they are eager to assist Starseeds in their personal and collective evolution.

One of the key aspects of deepening this relationship is learning to trust the guidance that is received. Galactic Guides operate on a frequency of unconditional love and are always working in alignment with the highest good of the Starseed. However, the guidance they offer may not always align with the immediate desires or expectations of the individual. It is important to remember that these guides see the bigger picture, and their wisdom often transcends the limitations of the human perspective.

Trusting the guidance of Galactic Guides requires a willingness to surrender control and allow the higher wisdom of the cosmos to lead the way. This can be challenging, especially when the guidance asks the Starseed to step outside of their comfort zone or make significant changes in their life. However, by following the guidance of their Galactic Guides, Starseeds often find that they are led toward experiences that accelerate their spiritual growth and align them more fully with their divine purpose.

Another important aspect of deepening the relationship with Galactic Guides is reciprocity. While these guides offer their support freely and unconditionally, the relationship is most fulfilling when it is balanced by an expression of gratitude and love. Starseeds can show their appreciation by taking time to honor their guides through rituals, offerings, or simply expressing gratitude during meditation. This act of giving back strengthens the bond between the Starseed and their guides, creating a harmonious exchange of energy.

The Role of Galactic Guides in Ascension

Galactic Guides are not only personal mentors to Starseeds; they also play a critical role in the broader ascension process. As Earth moves through its current phase of transformation, Galactic Guides are working closely with Starseeds to anchor higher-dimensional frequencies on the planet. These guides are deeply invested in the success of Earth's ascension, as it is part of a larger cosmic plan that affects multiple star systems and dimensions.

Through their connection with Starseeds, Galactic Guides transmit high-vibrational energy, wisdom, and healing that contribute to the collective awakening of humanity. They assist Starseeds in stepping into their roles as leaders, healers, and way-showers, helping to activate the global grid of light that is essential for planetary ascension. Many Starseeds are called to work directly with their Galactic Guides in service to the collective, whether through healing work, teaching, or sharing spiritual knowledge.

In times of great planetary shifts, Galactic Guides often work with Starseeds to stabilize the energies of the Earth and assist in the integration of new frequencies. They may provide specific instructions on how to work with the Cosmic Flame or other ascension tools to facilitate the transition into higher-dimensional consciousness. As trusted allies, Galactic Guides are always available to offer support, guidance, and protection as humanity moves through this transformative period.

Connecting with Galactic Guides and star beings is an essential aspect of the Starseed's ascension journey. These guides offer wisdom, love, and guidance from higher dimensions, helping Starseeds to navigate the challenges of spiritual evolution and align with their divine purpose. By opening the channels of communication, deepening the relationship, and trusting in the guidance received, Starseeds can forge a powerful connection with their Galactic Guides, ultimately contributing to the collective ascension of humanity and the Earth.

Developing a Relationship with Cosmic Guides

As Starseeds progress on their ascension journey, establishing and nurturing a relationship with their Cosmic Guides becomes a pivotal aspect of their spiritual evolution. These guides, who exist across higher dimensions, are dedicated to assisting Starseeds in unlocking their fullest potential. Developing a clear and profound connection with them not only empowers the Starseed's personal journey but also allows them to receive wisdom, support, and insights from realms far beyond the limitations of the physical world.

The first step in building this relationship is understanding the nature of Cosmic Guides themselves. These guides, often hailing from advanced civilizations such as the Pleiades, Sirius, or Arcturus, are evolved beings that operate within a framework of unity consciousness and unconditional love. They are often assigned to Starseeds before incarnation, guiding them throughout their earthly experiences. Unlike traditional spirit guides, who tend to focus on everyday life challenges and spiritual lessons, Cosmic Guides are specifically attuned to the Starseed's galactic heritage and soul mission. They help Starseeds remember their cosmic origins, navigate the ascension process, and activate latent soul gifts that are necessary for both personal and planetary evolution.

Opening the Pathways of Communication

While Cosmic Guides are always present, many Starseeds are unaware of how to consciously communicate with them. Developing this connection begins with intention and the cultivation of openness. Setting a clear intention to connect with one's Cosmic Guides is the first step in creating a bridge between the dimensions. Intentions act as energetic signals, inviting these higher-dimensional beings into the Starseed's conscious awareness.

A simple practice to begin this connection is meditation, which quiets the mind and raises the individual's vibrational frequency to a level more aligned with that of the Cosmic Guides. During meditation, Starseeds can visualize themselves surrounded by a field of white or golden light, which acts as a protective barrier and a beacon for their guides. As they settle into a state of relaxation, they can mentally or verbally invite their Cosmic Guides to come forward and make their presence known. While the communication may not be immediate, Starseeds are encouraged to trust the process, knowing that their guides will respond in divine timing.

In addition to meditation, dreamwork can be a powerful tool for connecting with Cosmic Guides. Many guides communicate through dreams, where the Starseed's conscious mind is relaxed, and access to higher dimensions is more fluid. Starseeds may experience vivid, otherworldly dreams or encounters with beings who seem familiar yet otherworldly. Keeping a dream journal is essential for tracking these experiences, as the symbols and messages received in dreams often contain important guidance.

As the Starseed deepens their connection with their guides, they may begin to notice synchronicities—meaningful coincidences that confirm the presence of their guides. For example, recurring numbers, symbols, or encounters with animals may all serve as signs that the guides are communicating. Trusting these subtle signs is crucial in building confidence in the relationship.

The Role of Trust and Patience

One of the greatest challenges Starseeds face in developing a relationship with their Cosmic Guides is overcoming doubt. The communication from guides often arrives in subtle, non-linear ways that the logical mind might dismiss. Trust is essential in this process. While Starseeds may yearn for clear and direct messages, it is important to recognize that the guides operate on frequencies of energy and intuition. The more a Starseed practices quieting the mind and attuning to the subtleties of the communication, the clearer the guidance becomes.

Patience is another critical aspect of this relationship. Unlike instant messages or linear conversations, communication with Cosmic Guides unfolds organically. Guides often work through energetic downloads or shifts in perspective that gradually align the Starseed with their higher path. Starseeds may receive a piece of guidance and not fully understand its significance until days or weeks later when circumstances in their life begin to reflect that wisdom. This process of unfolding should be embraced with patience, allowing the relationship with the guides to deepen naturally over time.

Trust is further solidified through small acts of confirmation. For example, after receiving a message from a guide during meditation or a dream, a Starseed might ask for a confirmation in their waking life. This could take the form of encountering a specific symbol, animal, or phrase that reinforces the original guidance. The more these confirmations occur, the more trust builds, and the stronger the relationship between the Starseed and their guides becomes.

Enhancing the Connection Through Ritual and Sacred Space

For many Starseeds, ritual plays an important role in developing a deeper connection with their Cosmic Guides. Creating a sacred space dedicated to communion with these beings can elevate the energy of the relationship and signal to the guides that the Starseed is ready to receive their guidance in a more structured way. This sacred space can be as simple or elaborate as the Starseed desires—a small altar with crystals, candles, or objects that resonate with their galactic heritage can serve as a focal point.

Incorporating sacred symbols and tools that resonate with the Starseed's galactic lineage can further amplify the connection. For example, some Starseeds feel a strong connection to the geometry of certain star systems or to specific light codes. Integrating these symbols into their sacred space, or working with crystals that carry high-vibrational frequencies (such as moldavite, clear quartz, or selenite), can enhance the energy field in which the guides operate.

Rituals such as lighting candles, burning incense, or playing high-frequency music during meditation or moments of reflection can help raise the vibration of the environment and the Starseed, making communication with the guides more fluid. Offering a regular time each day or week for this communion signals to the guides that the Starseed is committed to the relationship, and over time, the communication becomes more consistent and profound.

Another powerful ritual for enhancing the connection with Cosmic Guides is writing. Starseeds may find that writing letters to their guides, expressing their thoughts, questions, and intentions, opens the door for deeper communication. Writing allows the Starseed to articulate their desires clearly, while also inviting the guides to respond. This can be particularly effective in combination with automatic writing, where the Starseed allows the words to flow without conscious control, often resulting in messages directly from the guides themselves.

Integrating Galactic Guidance into Everyday Life

Once the connection with Cosmic Guides is established, the next phase involves integrating their guidance into everyday life. While communication with guides often feels sacred and otherworldly, it is important to remember that the purpose of this relationship is to assist the Starseed in navigating their human experience. Galactic Guides offer wisdom that can be applied to all areas of life, from relationships and career choices to health and spiritual growth.

The key to integrating this guidance is remaining present and open to the flow of information. As Starseeds move through their daily lives, they may receive intuitive nudges, sudden insights, or even feelings of comfort or assurance during challenging moments. These are all signs that the guides are offering their support. By honoring these small moments and acting on the guidance received, Starseeds allow the wisdom of their guides to become a living, breathing part of their reality.

Over time, the relationship with Cosmic Guides evolves into a partnership where the Starseed can draw upon their guidance with ease and confidence. Whether making a major life decision or simply seeking comfort during a difficult day, the Starseed knows that their guides are always available, ready to offer support and insight from higher realms.

The ultimate goal of developing a relationship with Cosmic Guides is to create a sense of co-creation with the cosmos. As the Starseed and their guides work together, they co-create a reality that is aligned with the Starseed's soul mission and the collective ascension of humanity. This relationship, rooted in love and unity, serves as a powerful reminder that Starseeds are never alone on their journey. They are always surrounded by a team of cosmic allies, ready to assist in every step of the ascension process.

Channeling Galactic Wisdom for Spiritual Growth

The process of channeling galactic wisdom is an extraordinary gift that offers Starseeds access to vast realms of cosmic knowledge and guidance. Channeling is not only a tool for spiritual growth, but also a bridge between dimensions, allowing Starseeds to align with the broader mission of global ascension while accelerating their personal journey of enlightenment.

At its core, channeling refers to the act of receiving and transmitting messages from higher-dimensional beings. These beings, often described as galactic guides or members of ascended civilizations, offer wisdom that transcends the limitations of the physical world. Unlike traditional forms of spiritual guidance that may focus on personal growth or earthbound challenges, galactic wisdom is often concerned with universal truths, multidimensional realities, and the evolution of consciousness. For Starseeds, this wisdom can serve as both a compass and a lifeline, helping them navigate the complexities of their spiritual awakening while offering profound insights into the nature of the cosmos.

The practice of channeling is not reserved for the spiritually advanced; it is an innate ability that can be developed with dedication and the right tools. As Starseeds begin to awaken to their cosmic origins, many will find that the urge to connect with higher realms becomes a natural part of their journey. However, the process of channeling galactic wisdom requires preparation, patience, and trust in the unseen.

Preparing to Channel: Raising Your Vibration

Before a Starseed can channel effectively, it is crucial to understand the role of frequency and vibration in the process. Galactic guides and higher-dimensional beings operate on frequencies that are far more refined and elevated than the dense, third-dimensional reality that humans typically inhabit. To access their wisdom, a Starseed must raise their own vibrational frequency to a level that aligns with these higher planes. This is achieved through various spiritual practices, each designed to purify the body, mind, and soul, and elevate the overall frequency of the individual.

Meditation remains one of the most effective methods for raising vibration. By stilling the mind and focusing on the breath, Starseeds can enter a state of deep relaxation where they become more receptive to subtle energies. During meditation, visualization techniques, such as imagining oneself surrounded by a golden or violet light, can further enhance the energetic field. This light acts as a protective shield and also signals to higher beings that the Starseed is ready and open for communication.

In addition to meditation, the use of sacred tools can support the raising of vibration. Crystals such as clear quartz, amethyst, and celestite are known to amplify spiritual energy and can be placed around the Starseed during their channeling sessions. Sound healing, whether through singing bowls, tuning forks, or chanting, can also raise the frequency of both the individual and the space in which they are working, making it easier for galactic guides to make contact.

Diet and lifestyle play a significant role in vibration as well. Starseeds are encouraged to consume high-vibrational foods —primarily plant-based, organic, and whole—while avoiding substances that lower their energy, such as processed foods, alcohol, and excessive caffeine. Physical activity, particularly yoga or practices that focus on the flow of energy, can also assist in elevating the frequency of the body and maintaining the balance necessary for successful channeling.

Initiating Galactic Communication: Opening the Channels

Once a Starseed has raised their vibration, they are ready to initiate communication with galactic beings. However, it is important to understand that channeling is not always an instantaneous process. Patience and trust are essential as the Starseed begins to open the channels of communication. Galactic guides communicate through energy, symbols, thoughts, and feelings rather than through direct, linear dialogue. Therefore, the Starseed must develop an acute sensitivity to these subtle forms of communication.

One effective technique for initiating communication is to begin each channeling session with an invocation. By setting a clear intention and calling upon their galactic guides, the Starseed creates a sacred space in which communication can occur. An invocation might sound like this: "I call upon my highest and most benevolent galactic guides to come forward at this time.

I open myself to receive the highest truth and wisdom for my spiritual growth and the collective ascension of humanity. May this communication be clear, loving, and aligned with the highest good."

After the invocation, it is important to sit in stillness and allow the energy to flow naturally. It may take time before the Starseed receives a clear message, but subtle shifts—such as a feeling of warmth, tingling, or even light pressure around the head or crown—often indicate that the connection has been made. At this point, the Starseed may begin to perceive thoughts, images, or even full sentences that seem to arrive from outside of themselves. Trusting in these impressions is key. Over time, as the relationship with the guides deepens, the clarity and frequency of the messages will increase.

Automatic writing is another powerful technique for channeling galactic wisdom. In this practice, the Starseed allows the hand to move freely across the page, without consciously controlling the words that appear. Often, messages from galactic guides will flow effortlessly through this method, bypassing the analytical mind. Keeping a dedicated journal for these communications is highly recommended, as it allows the Starseed to reflect on the guidance they receive and track their spiritual progress over time.

Integrating Galactic Wisdom into Daily Life

Receiving wisdom from galactic guides is a profound experience, but the true value of this communication lies in its integration into daily life. Galactic wisdom is not meant to remain abstract or esoteric; it is a living force that can be applied to the Starseed's everyday experiences, decisions, and growth. This wisdom often provides insights into how to navigate personal challenges, relationships, and even the broader mission of service to humanity's ascension.

One of the primary teachings that Starseeds often receive from their galactic guides is the importance of unity consciousness. Galactic wisdom frequently emphasizes the interconnectedness of all beings, regardless of their physical location or dimension. As Starseeds begin to understand this truth on a deeper level, they are encouraged to apply it by cultivating compassion, empathy, and service in their interactions with others. Acts of kindness, non-judgment, and the conscious intention to uplift others are practical ways to live out this galactic truth in everyday life.

Galactic guides also provide guidance on the Starseed's personal mission. Many Starseeds are drawn to specific areas of service, such as healing, teaching, or environmental work, and the wisdom they receive from their guides often aligns with these soul callings. For example, a Starseed who is called to be a healer may receive specific instructions on how to enhance their healing abilities or be guided toward new modalities of energy work. Likewise, a Starseed drawn to teaching might be given insights on how to communicate complex spiritual concepts in a way that is accessible and transformative for others.

Another aspect of integrating galactic wisdom involves the application of higher-dimensional teachings to the Starseed's spiritual practice. Guides often provide specific instructions on meditation techniques, energy work, or rituals that can accelerate the Starseed's ascension. For example, a guide might suggest a particular meditation for clearing the chakras or offer a technique for expanding the light body. By incorporating these teachings into their daily spiritual routine, the Starseed not only enhances their personal growth but also deepens their connection to the galactic realms.

The Role of Discernment

As Starseeds develop their channeling abilities, the importance of discernment cannot be overstated. Not all beings who communicate from higher dimensions have the Starseed's highest good in mind. It is essential for Starseeds to establish clear boundaries and only allow communication with beings who align with the frequency of love, unity, and divine truth. Invoking protection through light or calling upon higher-level guides such as archangels can ensure that the Starseed remains aligned with the highest sources of wisdom.

Discernment also applies to the messages themselves. While galactic wisdom can be profound, it is important for Starseeds to critically evaluate the guidance they receive and ensure that it resonates deeply with their soul. If a message feels out of alignment or creates fear, it may be necessary to pause and reassess the connection. Trusting one's intuition is the key to navigating this process and ensuring that the wisdom received is authentic and beneficial.

Channeling as a Path to Collective Ascension

Ultimately, the wisdom channeled from galactic guides serves not only the individual Starseed but also the broader mission of collective ascension. Galactic guides work tirelessly to support humanity's evolution, and as more Starseeds awaken to their cosmic origins, the collective frequency of the planet rises. By channeling and applying galactic wisdom, Starseeds play a vital role in anchoring higher-dimensional knowledge on Earth, accelerating the ascension of the entire human race.

Through dedication, trust, and an open heart, Starseeds can cultivate a profound relationship with their galactic guides, drawing upon their wisdom to fuel both personal and planetary transformation. As these celestial connections deepen, the Starseed becomes a living conduit for galactic truth, helping to bridge the gap between dimensions and guiding humanity toward a future rooted in unity, love, and higher consciousness.

Advanced Galactic Communication and Mastery

As Starseeds continue their ascension journey, the ability to communicate with higher-dimensional beings evolves from a nascent skill into a profound mastery. Advanced galactic communication goes far beyond receiving occasional messages or intuitive insights; it involves becoming a clear conduit for multidimensional wisdom, participating in higher councils, and accessing vast reservoirs of cosmic knowledge.

The process of advanced communication begins with the recognition that higher-dimensional beings do not operate within the limitations of time and space that we experience in the third dimension. They exist in a realm of fluid consciousness where past, present, and future merge, and where thoughts, energies, and intentions manifest instantaneously. This fluidity can be challenging for those just starting their communication journey, but for advanced practitioners, it becomes a key to unlocking deeper layers of understanding. With practice, Starseeds learn to navigate these expansive energies, attuning themselves to the subtle frequencies of different galactic councils, wisdom keepers, and even interstellar collectives that hold specific knowledge for Earth's ascension.

Cultivating Galactic Sensitivity

Advanced communication with galactic beings requires a heightened level of sensitivity to both energetic frequencies and the vibrational shifts that accompany interdimensional contact. This sensitivity is cultivated over time through consistent spiritual practice and a deep commitment to personal purification. Starseeds must clear their own energetic fields of lower vibrations, mental clutter, and emotional distortions that can block clear communication. A cluttered mind or emotional instability can act as static, distorting the messages received or blocking the subtle nuances of higher-dimensional communication.

To cultivate this galactic sensitivity, Starseeds should engage in regular energetic clearing practices, including deep meditation, energy work, and light body activation. These practices help refine the Starseed's vibrational frequency, allowing them to become more attuned to the subtle shifts in energy that signal the presence of galactic beings. Meditation that focuses on expanding awareness into multidimensional realms—such as the use of visualization to travel through stargates, or connecting with the infinite cosmos—can greatly enhance this sensitivity. The goal is to extend one's consciousness beyond the limitations of the physical body and tune into the expansive field of universal consciousness where all information is accessible.

Additionally, maintaining a strong and clear connection to the Earth is crucial, even as one explores higher realms. Grounding practices such as walking in nature, working with grounding crystals like black tourmaline, or engaging in breathwork that anchors the energy body to the Earth, help prevent the disorientation that can sometimes accompany advanced interdimensional work. Galactic guides often emphasize the importance of being both rooted in the physical and expansive in consciousness. This duality ensures that the Starseed can receive advanced information while still applying it effectively within the physical realm.

Accessing Higher Councils and Galactic Libraries

One of the hallmarks of advanced galactic communication is the ability to access higher councils of light and galactic libraries of wisdom. These councils consist of highly evolved beings—many of whom have ascended beyond the need for physical form—who are dedicated to the upliftment of sentient beings across the universe. For Starseeds, gaining access to these councils can provide profound insights into their soul mission, the collective ascension process, and the larger galactic shifts that are occurring within the universe.

Accessing these councils requires more than just raising one's vibration; it requires alignment with the purpose of service. Starseeds who seek to enter the higher councils must do so with the intention of serving the greater good, not for personal gain or egoic validation. The councils communicate only with those who are ready to embody the teachings they receive and who will use this knowledge for the benefit of others. This alignment is a key factor in gaining permission to access these interdimensional gatherings.

Galactic libraries, also known as the Akashic Records of the cosmos, are another resource for advanced Starseeds. These libraries are vast repositories of information that contain the knowledge of every soul, every civilization, and every event across time and space. While many Starseeds may have accessed the Akashic Records on a personal level, advanced practitioners can expand their access to the galactic level, retrieving information about universal laws, intergalactic relationships, and even the collective karmic imprints of entire civilizations. This information can be used to inform the Starseed's work on Earth, providing guidance on how to assist humanity during pivotal shifts in consciousness.

The key to accessing these galactic libraries is trust. Often, the information received may not make logical sense to the rational mind, as it operates on a higher frequency of understanding. Starseeds must trust in the information they are being given, allowing time for the knowledge to integrate and become clearer. Journaling, meditative reflection, and intuitive inquiry can all help in processing this advanced information and making it applicable to Earth's ascension journey.

Direct Downloads of Galactic Wisdom

As Starseeds develop their abilities in advanced galactic communication, they may experience what is commonly referred to as "direct downloads" of wisdom. These downloads occur when a Starseed is able to open their consciousness wide enough to receive large amounts of information directly from higher-dimensional beings or interstellar collectives. Unlike traditional channeling, where information is delivered in a linear manner (such as through spoken or written words), direct downloads come in the form of energetic packets of information that are received instantaneously. These downloads are often multidimensional, containing layers of understanding that unfold over time.

Direct downloads can be overwhelming for those unaccustomed to the intensity of the experience. It is common for Starseeds to feel disoriented, fatigued, or emotionally charged after receiving a download. However, with practice, the Starseed can learn to manage the influx of energy and integrate the information without becoming overwhelmed. Grounding is essential after receiving a download, as it helps anchor the information into the physical body and allows the Starseed to process it more effectively.

The content of these downloads can vary widely, from personal guidance on the Starseed's path to large-scale information about planetary shifts, galactic alignments, and the role of humanity in the cosmic plan. Starseeds receiving direct downloads often feel a deep sense of responsibility to act on the information, as it is often imbued with a sense of urgency or purpose.

Mastering Galactic Communication for Global Ascension

At the highest levels of galactic communication, Starseeds are not only receiving wisdom for their own spiritual growth but are also acting as conduits for planetary and collective ascension. As humanity continues its evolutionary journey, the role of Starseeds becomes increasingly important in anchoring higher-dimensional frequencies on Earth. Galactic beings, many of whom have overseen humanity's progress for millennia, work closely with advanced Starseeds to bring through the information and energies necessary for this planetary shift.

Advanced galactic communication often involves working directly with these beings to channel energies that assist in stabilizing the Earth's energy grid, aligning humanity with higher timelines, and dissolving outdated karmic imprints that have kept the planet in lower vibrations. Starseeds may be called upon to lead global meditations, participate in energy work that supports the Earth's ascension, or even facilitate communication between galactic councils and human leaders as humanity prepares for deeper integration into the galactic community.

This level of communication requires not only personal mastery but also a commitment to the collective. Starseeds must move beyond personal agendas and align themselves fully with the mission of planetary ascension. Galactic beings who work with advanced Starseeds often remind them of the sacred responsibility they carry: to serve as bridges between the human experience and the broader galactic family.

Becoming a Galactic Conduit

Advanced galactic communication is a path of mastery that requires dedication, humility, and an unwavering commitment to the ascension process. As Starseeds refine their abilities to communicate with higher-dimensional beings, they become conduits for the wisdom, energy, and love that the galaxy has to offer. This communication is not about ego or personal achievement; it is about stepping into a role of service, anchoring higher truths, and assisting in the awakening of humanity.

For those who feel the call to pursue this path, the rewards are profound. Not only does galactic communication offer unparalleled spiritual growth, but it also deepens the Starseed's connection to the universe, reminding them of their place within the cosmic tapestry. As Starseeds step into this role of mastery, they become vital links in the ascension chain, holding the light of the cosmos within their hearts and shining it forth for all to see. Through their dedication, they help pave the way for humanity's reunion with its galactic family and the fulfillment of its divine potential.

ASCENSION TOOLS AND PRACTICES

Tools for Starseed Awakening

As Starseeds embark on their journey of awakening and spiritual evolution, tools serve as sacred aids in amplifying their connection to the Cosmic Flame. These tools, both physical and energetic, offer support in aligning with higher dimensions, activating dormant codes within their DNA, and facilitating a deeper relationship with the cosmic forces guiding their ascension.

The process of Starseed awakening is often accompanied by a heightened sensitivity to energy, an increased awareness of cosmic forces, and a deep desire to reconnect with one's galactic origins. In these early stages of awakening, many Starseeds experience profound shifts in their perception of reality, often leading to feelings of disorientation or uncertainty. It is during these moments of vulnerability that the use of spiritual tools becomes invaluable. These tools not only help ground and center the individual but also serve as gateways to higher realms, providing clarity, protection, and guidance along the ascension path.

Crystals: Amplifiers of Cosmic Energy

Crystals have long been revered as powerful conduits of energy, holding within them the vibrational frequencies of the Earth and the cosmos. For Starseeds, crystals act as amplifiers of the Cosmic Flame, helping to focus their intentions and channel higher frequencies of light into their energy bodies. Each crystal carries a unique vibration that can assist in different aspects of the awakening process, from clearing energetic blockages to enhancing communication with higher-dimensional beings.

For instance, amethyst is known for its ability to enhance spiritual awareness and intuition, making it an ideal crystal for Starseeds seeking to deepen their connection to their galactic guides. Clear quartz, often referred to as the "master healer," can be used to amplify energy and intentions, making it a versatile tool for all stages of spiritual growth. Moldavite, a crystal formed from meteorite impacts, is especially potent for Starseeds, as its extraterrestrial origins resonate with the frequencies of the cosmos, aiding in the acceleration of personal and planetary ascension.

Crystals can be used in various ways to support awakening. Starseeds can meditate with crystals, placing them on key energy points in the body such as the third eye or heart chakra to facilitate the flow of cosmic energy. They can also be worn as jewelry or placed in their environment to create an energetic grid that supports spiritual growth. It's important for Starseeds to cleanse and program their crystals regularly, as these powerful tools absorb and amplify the energy around them.

Sound: The Language of Creation

Sound is another potent tool in the awakening process, as it taps directly into the vibrational essence of the universe. Everything in existence is in a constant state of vibration, and sound provides a direct pathway to align with the higher frequencies of the cosmos. For Starseeds, working with sound can help harmonize their energy bodies, clear energetic blockages, and activate dormant codes within their DNA that are essential for ascension.

Sound healing instruments such as tuning forks, crystal bowls, and Tibetan singing bowls resonate with specific frequencies that correspond to the energy centers in the body. When these frequencies are played, they create a ripple effect throughout the energetic field, restoring balance and aligning the Starseed's vibration with higher dimensional realms. For example, a crystal singing bowl tuned to the frequency of the heart chakra can assist in opening the heart space, allowing for greater receptivity to love, compassion, and higher guidance.

Beyond instruments, the human voice itself is a powerful tool for awakening. Chanting mantras or sacred sounds, such as "OM," carries vibrational energy that aligns the individual with the frequency of the universe. Light language, a form of vocal expression that transcends the limitations of human language, is another potent tool for Starseeds. This cosmic language, often channeled from higher-dimensional beings, bypasses the rational mind and communicates directly with the soul, activating deep healing and transformation.

Starseeds can incorporate sound into their spiritual practice by creating daily rituals that involve chanting, toning, or playing sound healing instruments. These practices not only raise their personal frequency but also help attune them to the subtle energies of their galactic guides, making communication clearer and more profound.

Sacred Geometry: Unlocking Divine Codes

Sacred geometry is the universal language of creation, found in everything from the structure of atoms to the spiraling galaxies. It serves as a visual representation of the Cosmic Flame, and for Starseeds, it holds the keys to unlocking dormant codes within their DNA and consciousness. Each geometric shape carries a specific frequency that resonates with the foundational principles of the universe, and working with these patterns can facilitate deep healing, spiritual activation, and alignment with the higher dimensions.

The Flower of Life, a symbol composed of overlapping circles, is one of the most well-known forms of sacred geometry. It represents the interconnectedness of all life and the infinite patterns of creation. Meditating on the Flower of Life can help Starseeds tap into the universal energy grid, enhancing their sense of unity with the cosmos and deepening their understanding of their role in the ascension process. The Merkabah, a three-dimensional geometric shape, is another powerful tool that Starseeds can use to activate their light body and travel between dimensions.

Starseeds can work with sacred geometry by incorporating these patterns into their meditation practice or by creating altars that feature these shapes. Visualizing themselves surrounded by the energy of these symbols can help align their energy bodies with higher vibrational frequencies and accelerate their spiritual awakening.

Working with Energy Grids and Portals

Energy grids and portals are natural structures that exist both within and around the Earth, acting as conduits for cosmic energy. For Starseeds, learning to work with these grids and portals is essential for their awakening, as it allows them to anchor higher-dimensional energies into the physical realm and access interdimensional information.

The Earth is crisscrossed by a network of ley lines, which are energetic highways that carry the planet's life force energy. Sacred sites, such as Stonehenge and the Great Pyramids, are located at the intersection points of these ley lines, acting as powerful energy centers where the veil between dimensions is thin. Starseeds who visit these sites can experience profound activations, as the energy of these locations amplifies their connection to the Cosmic Flame and their galactic heritage.

Beyond the Earth, there are interdimensional portals that allow for communication and travel between different realms. These portals are often located in high-vibrational areas and can be accessed through meditation or energy work. Starseeds who are attuned to these portals can use them to receive downloads of cosmic information, travel to other dimensions, or even communicate with higher-dimensional beings.

Starseeds can begin working with energy grids and portals by meditating on sacred sites or visualizing themselves connecting with the Earth's ley lines. Creating an energetic grid in their own space using crystals or sacred geometry can also help amplify their connection to these cosmic energies, allowing them to access higher realms from the comfort of their own home.

Integrating Tools into Daily Practice

While the tools mentioned above are powerful in their own right, their true effectiveness lies in the consistency and intention behind their use. For Starseeds, awakening is not a singular event but an ongoing process that requires regular practice and dedication. By integrating these tools into their daily spiritual routines, Starseeds can accelerate their ascension journey, clear energetic blockages, and deepen their connection to the Cosmic Flame.

It's important for Starseeds to approach these tools with

reverence and respect, understanding that they are sacred aids in their spiritual evolution. Cleansing tools regularly—whether it's crystals, sound instruments, or energy grids—ensures that they remain attuned to the Starseed's energy and the higher frequencies they seek to access. Intentional use, coupled with gratitude, amplifies the tools' power, making them potent allies in the journey toward ascension.

The tools available to Starseeds during their awakening process are vast and varied, each offering unique support in their spiritual growth. Whether working with crystals, sound, sacred geometry, or energy grids, these tools help bridge the gap between the physical and the cosmic, enhancing the Starseed's ability to align with the higher dimensions. As they continue to use these tools with intention and dedication, Starseeds will find themselves increasingly attuned to the cosmic energies guiding their path, unlocking the full potential of their soul and its divine purpose. Through this sacred process, they become living embodiments of the Cosmic Flame, radiating light and wisdom to the world.

Advanced Crystal Grids and Cosmic Activation

Crystals have long been revered as conduits of higher energies, ancient tools used across cultures and dimensions for healing, protection, and spiritual awakening. For Starseeds, crystals are more than just material objects—they are extensions of the cosmic forces that shape the universe, holding within them vibrational frequencies that resonate with higher realms. The creation and use of crystal grids, in particular, offer Starseeds the opportunity to amplify their connection to the Cosmic Flame and activate spiritual power on a planetary level.

As Starseeds move deeper into their ascension journey, the use of crystal grids transcends simple meditation or healing practices. It becomes a means of aligning with the Earth's energy matrix and the larger cosmic web, allowing for a profound connection to both planetary and galactic forces. Crystal grids serve as blueprints for cosmic activation, tapping into the sacred geometry that underpins creation and channeling high-frequency energies into the physical plane. These advanced grids are not only for personal healing and transformation but also for collective ascension, as they can be used to awaken dormant energies within the Earth and support the awakening of humanity.

The Power of Crystals in Cosmic Alignment

Crystals are born from the Earth's womb, forged over millions of years through immense pressure and heat. This process imbues them with the frequencies of the planet, making them ideal tools for grounding cosmic energies into the physical realm. Each crystal carries a unique energetic signature, resonating with different aspects of the human energy body and the planetary grid. For Starseeds, working with these natural powerhouses enhances their ability to connect with higher-dimensional beings and energies, as well as align their own energy bodies with the Cosmic Flame.

However, in the context of crystal grids, the focus shifts from individual crystals to the synergy created by their collective arrangement. Crystal grids are sacred patterns, often based on principles of sacred geometry, that amplify the energetic properties of the crystals used. When arranged with intention, these grids become powerful portals of energy, capable of transmitting cosmic frequencies and opening the way for spiritual activation on a profound level.

The foundation of any crystal grid is the central crystal, which acts as the anchor point for the energy being summoned. This crystal is typically larger or of a higher vibrational frequency, such as a quartz point or a piece of selenite. Around this central crystal, supporting crystals are placed in geometric patterns that correspond to specific frequencies or intentions. Each crystal within the grid serves as a node, transmitting energy to the surrounding crystals and creating a network of vibrational resonance.

Creating Crystal Grids for Cosmic Activation

For Starseeds ready to explore the advanced use of crystal grids, it's essential to understand that the energy of these grids extends far beyond the physical. When properly attuned, a crystal grid becomes a bridge between dimensions, allowing Starseeds to channel cosmic energies into the Earth's energy field and their own spiritual practice. The key to this process is the alignment of the grid with sacred geometry, the universal language of creation that governs the movement of energy throughout the cosmos.

Sacred geometry refers to specific geometric patterns found in all aspects of life, from the spiral of a seashell to the structure of galaxies. These patterns are reflections of the divine order and serve as templates for energetic manifestation. When a crystal grid is arranged according to the principles of sacred geometry, it resonates with the underlying structure of the universe, allowing for a more powerful flow of cosmic energy.

One of the most common patterns used in crystal grids is the Flower of Life, a geometric design composed of overlapping circles that represents the interconnectedness of all life. The

Flower of Life serves as a potent template for cosmic activation, as it mirrors the structure of the universe itself. By arranging crystals in this pattern, Starseeds can tap into the universal grid and align their energy with the higher dimensions. Other sacred geometric patterns, such as the Metatron's Cube or the Sri Yantra, can also be used for specific activations, depending on the intention of the grid.

When creating an advanced crystal grid, it's important to approach the process with reverence and intention. The grid should be placed in a space that is energetically clear, and Starseeds should take time to cleanse and program their crystals before use. This can be done through meditation, visualization, or sound healing, allowing the crystals to vibrate at their highest potential.

Activating the Crystal Grid

Once the grid has been constructed, the process of activation begins. Activation is the moment when the grid transitions from a static arrangement of crystals to a living, energetic entity. To activate the grid, Starseeds must infuse it with their intention, calling forth the energies they wish to summon and align with. This can be done through visualization, mantra, or connecting with higher-dimensional beings such as galactic guides.

One method of activation involves using a clear quartz point or a wand to trace the lines of the grid, connecting the energy of each crystal. As this is done, the Starseed can visualize light flowing through the grid, creating a web of energy that radiates out into the Earth's energy field. It's important to remain present and focused during this process, as the intention behind the activation determines the frequency of the energy that will be transmitted.

For cosmic activation, Starseeds may also call upon specific star systems or galactic guides to infuse the grid with their energy.

For example, those working with the Pleiades or Sirius can invite these higher-dimensional beings to amplify the grid's energy and align it with their frequencies. In doing so, the grid becomes not only a tool for personal ascension but a portal through which cosmic wisdom and energy can flow into the Earth plane.

Using Crystal Grids for Planetary and Collective Ascension

The role of Starseeds in the collective ascension process extends beyond personal awakening. As channels of the Cosmic Flame, Starseeds have the ability to work with the Earth's energy grid, facilitating the planet's ascension into higher dimensions. Crystal grids serve as a powerful tool in this process, as they allow Starseeds to anchor cosmic frequencies into the Earth's energy matrix and awaken dormant energies within the planetary grid.

One of the most potent ways to use crystal grids for planetary activation is by aligning them with the Earth's ley lines. Ley lines are energy pathways that crisscross the planet, connecting sacred sites such as Stonehenge, the Great Pyramids, and Machu Picchu. These sites are vortex points where the Earth's energy is especially strong, and they serve as portals for higher-dimensional energies to enter the physical realm. By placing crystal grids at these vortex points, Starseeds can amplify the flow of energy along the ley lines, awakening the global grid of light and accelerating the planet's ascension process.

It's important for Starseeds to work with intention and integrity when using crystal grids for planetary activation. The energy summoned through these grids is potent, and it must be used for the highest good of all beings. Starseeds can also work in groups to create collective grids, combining their intentions to generate even greater waves of energy. These collective grids can be placed at sacred sites, or smaller grids can be connected energetically through meditation and visualization, creating a global network of light.

Crystal Grids and Galactic Portals

In addition to working with the Earth's energy grid, crystal grids can be used to open galactic portals, allowing for communication and travel between dimensions. Galactic portals are energy gateways that connect the Earth to other star systems and higher-dimensional realms. By aligning a crystal grid with specific star frequencies, Starseeds can open these portals and receive downloads of cosmic wisdom, guidance, and energy from their galactic counterparts.

To open a galactic portal, Starseeds must first attune their grid to the frequency of the star system they wish to connect with. This can be done through visualization, meditation, or using crystals that resonate with the desired frequency. For example, those wishing to connect with the Pleiades may use blue kyanite or larimar, while those working with Sirius may use lapis lazuli or moldavite. Once the grid is aligned, the Starseed can call upon their galactic guides to open the portal and transmit their energy through the grid.

As the portal opens, the Starseed may experience a shift in consciousness, as they attune to the higher-dimensional frequencies flowing through the grid. These experiences can be profound, offering deep insights into the nature of the universe and the Starseed's role in the ascension process. It's important to remain grounded during these experiences, as the influx of cosmic energy can be overwhelming if not properly integrated.

Crystal grids are powerful tools for Starseeds, offering the opportunity to work with the energies of the Earth and the cosmos to facilitate personal and planetary ascension. Through the use of sacred geometry, intention, and alignment with higher-dimensional frequencies, these grids become portals of transformation, amplifying the flow of cosmic energy and awakening the dormant codes within the Earth and humanity. As Starseeds continue to explore the advanced use of crystal grids, they will find themselves increasingly aligned with their cosmic purpose, radiating the light of the Cosmic Flame for the benefit of all beings.

Sacred Sound and Light Codes for Ascension

Sound and light, both integral to the fabric of existence, hold the key to deeper realms of spiritual transformation and ascension. For Starseeds, these elements are more than mere vibrations; they are cosmic tools, fundamental frequencies that carry the wisdom of the universe. Through sound healing and light codes, Starseeds can access higher dimensions, activate dormant DNA, and align with the energies necessary for their spiritual evolution.

At the core of all existence, both sound and light represent the universal language of creation. Sound is the vibrational force that permeates everything, while light codes are the visual representations of divine frequencies. Together, they form the symphony of creation that echoes throughout the cosmos. These sacred tools have been used by advanced civilizations and higher-dimensional beings for eons to facilitate healing, transformation, and spiritual ascension. Whether through mantras, sound frequencies, or light activations, Starseeds can harness these energies to accelerate their journey toward higher consciousness.

The Role of Sound in Spiritual Ascension

Sound is vibration, and vibration is the fundamental essence of all matter and energy. From the resonant hum of the Earth's Schumann frequency to the cosmic sound of the OM, every aspect of the universe is composed of vibratory patterns. In the context of ascension, sound serves as a bridge between the material and spiritual worlds, a force that can break through energetic barriers and unlock deeper levels of consciousness.

For Starseeds, sound healing becomes a powerful practice that goes beyond relaxation or stress relief—it becomes a vehicle for spiritual awakening and transformation. Ancient civilizations such as the Atlanteans, Egyptians, and Lemurians were well-versed in the use of sound as a healing and ascension tool, using tuning forks, crystal bowls, and vocal toning to raise vibrational frequencies. The resonance created by these sounds has the ability to clear energetic blockages, align the chakras, and activate dormant strands of DNA.

In modern sound healing practices, Starseeds can use instruments such as Tibetan singing bowls, crystal bowls, tuning forks, and gongs to create harmonic vibrations that resonate with the body's energy centers. These sounds interact with the body's vibrational field, helping to shift energy blockages and bring the body, mind, and spirit into alignment. Each instrument produces a specific frequency that corresponds to different chakras and energy centers, promoting healing on physical, emotional, and spiritual levels.

However, beyond external instruments, the human voice remains one of the most potent tools for sound healing and ascension. The act of vocal toning—producing sustained vocal sounds—can generate powerful resonances within the body, facilitating the release of trapped emotions, activating dormant DNA, and connecting Starseeds to higher-dimensional frequencies. Chanting sacred mantras such as "OM" or "AH" can activate the pineal gland, the seat of spiritual awakening, and open the gateway to higher realms.

The specific use of solfeggio frequencies is another powerful way to work with sound for ascension. These frequencies are thought to carry divine healing properties, and each tone resonates with different aspects of the energetic body. For instance, the 528 Hz frequency is known as the "Miracle Tone" and is associated with DNA repair, while the 396 Hz frequency is used for releasing fear and guilt. Starseeds can incorporate these frequencies into their meditation or sound healing practice to raise their vibrational frequency and support their journey toward higher consciousness.

The Language of Light Codes

While sound serves as the vibrational force that moves through the physical and etheric bodies, light codes are the visual representation of higher-dimensional energies that activate the spiritual body. Light codes, often experienced in meditation, dreams, or visionary states, are intricate geometric patterns or symbols that carry information from higher realms. These codes bypass the rational mind and speak directly to the soul, unlocking memories of one's cosmic origins and activating latent spiritual abilities.

Light codes are more than just abstract symbols; they are living energy fields that carry the vibration of specific star systems, galactic frequencies, or divine beings. When a Starseed receives light codes, either through meditation, artwork, or light language transmission, these codes begin to work within their energy field, catalyzing deep spiritual transformations. They can activate dormant DNA strands, clear karmic imprints, and help integrate higher-dimensional energies into the physical body.

Many Starseeds experience light codes as geometric shapes, symbols, or colors that appear during deep meditation or dream states. These codes often resonate with the individual on a soul level, triggering memories of their star origins or past lives in higher dimensions. The sacred geometry of these codes holds the blueprint of creation, mirroring the structure of the universe itself. As Starseeds integrate these codes, they are aligning their energy bodies with the divine order, facilitating their ascension process.

Light language is another powerful tool for receiving and transmitting light codes. This multidimensional language is not bound by linear syntax or vocabulary; instead, it is a direct transmission of higher-dimensional frequencies in the form of sound, symbols, or gestures. Many Starseeds find themselves spontaneously speaking, writing, or drawing light language as they connect with their higher self or galactic guides. While the conscious mind may not understand the words or symbols, the soul recognizes and integrates the energetic frequency behind the language.

For those new to working with light codes, it's essential to approach these experiences with an open heart and mind. Light codes may come in many forms—through visualizations, energy transmissions, or light language—and each Starseed will have their unique way of receiving and integrating them. The key is to trust the process and allow the codes to work within the energy field, even if the conscious mind does not fully understand their meaning.

Integrating Sound and Light for Ascension

As Starseeds progress on their spiritual path, the integration of sound and light becomes a potent means of accelerating the ascension process. When sound and light are combined, they create a harmonious field of energy that resonates with the soul's highest potential. Sound frequencies act as the catalyst, while light codes serve as the blueprint for transformation, together facilitating deep spiritual healing and activation.

One of the most powerful ways to integrate sound and light is through sacred ceremonies or meditative practices that combine vocal toning, light language, and visualization of light codes. Starseeds can create sacred spaces where they chant or tone specific mantras while visualizing or drawing light codes that correspond to their intentions. For example, a Starseed seeking to activate their third eye chakra might chant the "OM" sound while visualizing a light code of the Sri Yantra, an ancient symbol associated with higher consciousness and spiritual awakening.

Group sound healing sessions are another way to amplify the power of sound and light integration. When Starseeds come together in a collective intention, the resonance of their combined voices or instruments creates a powerful energetic field that allows for deeper activation and healing. As the group chants, tones, or speaks light language, each participant receives the vibrational frequencies necessary for their ascension, while also contributing to the collective energy field.

Additionally, Starseeds can work with specific sacred sounds or frequencies, such as solfeggio tones or crystal bowls, in combination with guided light code visualizations. As they play the sound frequencies, they can visualize the corresponding light codes entering their energy field, clearing blockages, and activating higher-dimensional energies. This practice can be done individually or in groups, depending on the intention and the level of activation desired.

Sacred sound and light codes are powerful tools that can facilitate profound spiritual growth and transformation. For Starseeds, working with these vibrational frequencies opens the gateway to higher consciousness, allowing for the integration of galactic wisdom, DNA activation, and alignment with the Cosmic Flame. As Starseeds embrace these ancient practices, they reconnect with their cosmic origins and step into their role as co-creators in the ascension of humanity and the planet.

The journey of sound and light is not merely about healing the body or clearing the mind; it is about awakening the soul to its highest potential. By integrating sound healing and light codes into their spiritual practice, Starseeds can access the deeper layers of their multidimensional self, unlocking the divine wisdom within and accelerating their ascension journey. In doing so, they become living embodiments of the Cosmic Flame, radiating light and harmony into the world and beyond.

Mastery of Ascension Technology and Tools

In the advanced stages of ascension, mastery over the tools and technologies that facilitate spiritual evolution becomes essential. These sacred instruments are not only symbolic but are also profoundly energetic in nature, serving as conduits for higher-dimensional frequencies. For Starseeds, the ability to harness and amplify these energies through the adept use of crystals, grids, light language, and other advanced tools is paramount. As the journey toward ascension reaches its most refined stages, these technologies provide the scaffolding for anchoring higher consciousness into physical reality.

In earlier stages of the ascension process, many of these tools are introduced as introductory aids, providing necessary energetic support and alignment for the individual Starseed. At this advanced level, however, the focus shifts from basic usage to mastery, where the practitioner is no longer merely receiving energy but actively shaping and directing it for both personal growth and the collective ascension process. This requires a deep understanding of the vibrational nuances of each tool, along with the capacity to work with them in dynamic, co-creative ways that push the boundaries of spiritual growth.

The Power of Crystal Technology

Crystals are among the most potent and ancient tools used in the ascension process, functioning as natural amplifiers of energy. Their internal lattice structure, composed of geometrically perfect formations, allows them to resonate with and magnify subtle energetic frequencies. For millennia, civilizations across the globe—from the Egyptians to the Atlanteans—have harnessed the energy of crystals for healing, spiritual growth, and the enhancement of consciousness. In the context of ascension mastery, the use of crystals goes far beyond simple meditation or energy clearing. It involves a deep resonance with the stones, a coalescence of intent, and a powerful collaboration between the Starseed and the crystalline realms.

One advanced practice in crystal technology is the creation and activation of crystal grids. These grids are sacred geometric arrangements of crystals that are designed to channel specific energetic frequencies. In earlier stages, grids may be used for personal healing or spiritual protection, but at this advanced level, their purpose evolves into something much more complex. Starseeds who have mastered the art of crystal grids can use these formations to open portals to higher dimensions, anchor light codes into the Earth's grid, and facilitate the collective awakening of humanity. This is done by selecting crystals that align with certain frequencies—such as quartz for clarity, selenite for divine connection, or labradorite for psychic protection—and arranging them in geometric patterns that amplify their combined energies.

The mastery of these grids also includes the ability to program the crystals with intention. By holding a clear vision or spiritual directive, the Starseed infuses the crystals with their own energy, allowing the stones to work in alignment with their desired outcome. This can include intentions for personal growth, planetary healing, or the activation of higher-dimensional consciousness. Over time, as the crystals are programmed and recharged, they become powerful allies in the Starseed's ascension toolkit.

The practice of working with crystals also extends to the use of specific stones for activating energy centers in the body. For instance, placing an amethyst crystal on the third eye during meditation can enhance intuition and spiritual sight, while grounding stones like black tourmaline can help stabilize and integrate the higher energies being accessed. Starseeds who have achieved mastery in this area understand that these stones are not passive tools but active participants in the spiritual process, working in harmony with their energy fields to promote balance, healing, and evolution.

Light Language and Advanced Energy Work

At this advanced stage, the mastery of ascension tools also includes working with light language—a multidimensional form of communication that transcends linear thought. Light language can be spoken, sung, drawn, or even gestured, and it serves as a direct transmission of higher-dimensional frequencies. When spoken or written, light language bypasses the conscious mind, delivering codes of light directly to the soul for activation and healing. Many Starseeds find that as they progress in their ascension journey, they begin to channel light language spontaneously, as it becomes a natural extension of their higher-dimensional self.

For those seeking mastery, working with light language involves developing the ability to consciously channel and direct this energy with purpose. This could be in the form of specific activations for themselves or others, using light language to unlock dormant DNA, clear karmic imprints, or facilitate collective healing. In many ways, light language functions like a spiritual technology, capable of transmitting vast amounts of information and energy in a compact, vibrational form. As such, it is a vital tool for those who are stepping into roles of leadership and healing within the ascension process.

In tandem with light language, advanced energy work becomes a cornerstone of ascension mastery. While earlier stages of the journey may focus on personal energy clearing and chakra alignment, this level of mastery requires the ability to work with complex energy fields, both within oneself and in the environment. This includes working with energy grids—both personal and planetary—and becoming attuned to the subtle shifts in frequency that occur as higher-dimensional energies are integrated into the Earth plane. Mastering these energies often involves practices such as advanced Reiki, meridian healing, or working with the Earth's ley lines, where the practitioner can influence and harmonize energy flows on both micro and macro levels.

The Integration of Sacred Geometry

Another critical tool in the ascension mastery toolkit is sacred geometry. Sacred geometric shapes, such as the Flower of Life, Metatron's Cube, and the Merkaba, are not just abstract symbols but are visual representations of the universal laws that govern the cosmos. These shapes carry the frequencies of creation itself, and by meditating on them or incorporating them into energy work, Starseeds can tap into the divine blueprint of existence.

At an advanced level, sacred geometry is integrated into almost every aspect of the ascension process. Crystal grids are often built upon the foundation of these geometric patterns, with stones arranged in ways that mirror the harmonic structures of the universe. Additionally, many Starseeds use sacred geometry as a meditation tool, visualizing these shapes within their energy field to activate different aspects of their light body or connect with higher-dimensional beings.

For example, the Merkaba, a three-dimensional star tetrahedron, is a powerful vehicle for ascension. By activating the Merkaba within one's energy field, a Starseed can access higher dimensions, receive downloads of cosmic information, and protect themselves from lower-vibrational energies. Advanced practitioners may also work with the Merkaba to facilitate astral travel or to merge their consciousness with the collective energy grid of the planet, aiding in the global ascension process.

Anchoring High-Frequency Energies

The ultimate goal of mastering ascension tools is to become an anchor for high-frequency energies, both within the individual's own life and within the collective energy field of the planet. As Starseeds ascend, their energetic vibration rises, and they become natural conduits for higher-dimensional frequencies. The tools and technologies discussed in this chapter are not only for personal use but are also for the benefit of the collective.

By mastering these tools, Starseeds can work to anchor these frequencies into the Earth's grid, helping to facilitate the shift into higher states of consciousness for all beings. This work is especially important as the planet undergoes its own ascension process, with new energies flooding in from higher-dimensional planes. Through their mastery, Starseeds become custodians of this shift, using their knowledge and tools to stabilize and support the planet and its inhabitants during this time of profound transformation.

The mastery of ascension tools is about far more than the simple use of crystals, grids, or light language. It is about becoming a co-creator with the universe, using these sacred technologies to shape reality, elevate consciousness, and facilitate the ascension of both the individual and the collective. As Starseeds step into this level of mastery, they embody the full potential of their cosmic heritage, serving as beacons of light in a rapidly evolving world.

BECOMING A COSMIC LEADER

Stepping into Your Role as a Starseed Leader

As the journey of ascension unfolds, the time inevitably comes when the Starseed is called to step into a leadership role. This is not merely about guiding others or teaching spiritual principles —it is a deeper calling that resonates from the very core of your cosmic origins. The role of a Starseed leader is sacred and purposeful, requiring both courage and humility. It is a responsibility that arises from the soul's wisdom, a knowledge that transcends lifetimes and dimensions. You are being asked to anchor the higher frequencies you've accessed into the collective consciousness of humanity, creating pathways for others to follow in their awakening.

For those who feel this call, it is often accompanied by a profound sense of both excitement and apprehension. The journey into leadership is not just about what you can give to others but also about what you must continually cultivate within yourself. It is an ever-deepening process of personal and spiritual growth, where mastery of your own energy, thoughts, and actions becomes the foundation for the impact you will have on the collective.

Awakening to Cosmic Leadership

The first step in stepping into your role as a Starseed leader is recognizing that this leadership is unlike any traditional notion of authority. It does not rely on hierarchy, control, or domination. Instead, it is a form of service that is rooted in love, empathy, and the sincere desire to elevate others. In this sense, leadership is more about embodying the higher frequencies you have integrated than it is about instructing others on how to follow. It is about being a living example of what it means to live from the heart, to align with the cosmic energies that are guiding the ascension of Earth and humanity.

Many Starseeds experience a "cosmic awakening" when they begin to understand their role as leaders. This often comes as a deep, inner knowing that emerges through meditation, dreams, or spontaneous moments of clarity. You may feel a sudden shift in your perception of the world, seeing not only the interconnectedness of all life but also your unique place within the grand cosmic tapestry. This awakening is the first sign that you are being called to step into a higher level of service.

Yet, the path to leadership is not without its challenges. Often, the greatest challenge comes from within—facing self-doubt, feelings of unworthiness, or the fear that you are not yet ready to guide others. These feelings are natural and are often part of the initiation process into leadership. It is important to remember that leadership is not about perfection but about authenticity.

You are not expected to have all the answers or to have reached a state of perfect enlightenment. Rather, your role is to walk the path of ascension alongside others, sharing your experiences, wisdom, and energy in ways that inspire and uplift.

Anchoring Leadership in the Cosmic Flame

The Cosmic Flame, as discussed throughout this book, is the guiding force of transformation, healing, and ascension. As a Starseed leader, your relationship with the Cosmic Flame becomes even more critical. It is through this sacred fire that you draw the strength, clarity, and spiritual wisdom necessary to fulfill your role as a leader. The Cosmic Flame is not only a tool for personal transformation but also a source of collective energy that can be harnessed to support the awakening of humanity.

Anchoring your leadership in the Cosmic Flame means continuously aligning with the highest frequencies of love, compassion, and divine wisdom. This requires regular spiritual practice, whether through meditation, energy work, or rituals that keep your connection to the Cosmic Flame strong and vibrant. As you deepen your connection with the flame, you will find that your capacity to lead with grace, authenticity, and wisdom expands naturally.

Moreover, the Cosmic Flame offers the spiritual protection needed for leadership. As you step into more visible roles, guiding others through their ascension journeys, you may encounter energetic challenges. These can include resistance from lower-vibrational forces, negative projections from others, or even internal doubts that arise as you navigate this path. The Cosmic Flame acts as a shield, allowing you to remain centered and aligned with your higher purpose, even in the face of difficulties.

Leadership Through Empowerment

One of the hallmarks of Starseed leadership is the ability to empower others. This is a form of leadership that does not seek to create followers but rather to awaken the innate power within each individual. It is about helping others recognize their own connection to the Cosmic Flame and guiding them in ways that foster their spiritual autonomy.

This approach to leadership is rooted in trust—trust in the divine intelligence of the universe and trust in the ability of each soul to find its way. As a leader, your role is to provide the tools, guidance, and support that others need to access their own inner wisdom. You are not there to dictate or control their spiritual journey, but to offer a space of love, compassion, and understanding where they can grow.

Empowerment also means being willing to share your own experiences authentically. While it is important to maintain spiritual discipline and alignment, there is no need to present yourself as infallible. In fact, sharing your struggles, doubts, and moments of vulnerability can be incredibly empowering for others. It reminds them that they are not alone in their challenges and that growth is a process that unfolds over time. By leading with transparency and vulnerability, you create a space where others feel safe to explore their own path.

Balancing Leadership and Personal Growth

Stepping into your role as a leader does not mean that your personal growth comes to an end. On the contrary, leadership often accelerates your own spiritual evolution. As you guide others, you are constantly challenged to deepen your understanding, to refine your practices, and to stay in alignment with your highest self.

It is essential to maintain a balance between giving to others and nurturing your own spiritual well-being. Leadership can be demanding, both energetically and emotionally, and it is easy to become depleted if you do not take time for self-care. Regularly connecting with the Cosmic Flame, setting healthy energetic boundaries, and creating time for your own spiritual practice are all crucial aspects of sustainable leadership.

Moreover, it is important to stay humble and open to learning. The path of ascension is infinite, and no matter how advanced you may become in your understanding, there is always more to explore, more to integrate, and more to master. Remaining a lifelong student of the universe ensures that your leadership remains grounded in curiosity, wonder, and continual growth.

Building Communities of Light

One of the most significant aspects of stepping into leadership is the role you play in building spiritual communities. These communities are essential for the collective ascension process, as they provide spaces where individuals can come together to support one another, share wisdom, and raise the planetary vibration. As a Starseed leader, you are called to create and nurture these communities, whether in physical spaces or through digital platforms.

Building a community of light is about creating a space where people feel seen, heard, and supported on their journey. It is about fostering an environment of inclusion, where each person's unique gifts and perspectives are honored. As a leader, your role is to hold the energetic space for the community, ensuring that it remains aligned with the higher frequencies of love, unity, and ascension.

In addition to creating these spaces, you are also responsible for guiding the community through collective spiritual practices, such as group meditations, healing circles, or planetary activation work. These gatherings are powerful opportunities to amplify the energy of the Cosmic Flame and to support the collective awakening of humanity. By leading with intention and clarity, you can create profound experiences that catalyze growth and transformation within your community.

Embracing Your Cosmic Role

Ultimately, stepping into your role as a Starseed leader is about embracing the full spectrum of your cosmic purpose. You are here not only to awaken yourself but to serve as a beacon of light for others. This is a sacred responsibility, one that requires you to remain in alignment with your highest self, to trust in the divine plan, and to lead with love, humility, and authenticity.

As you walk this path, remember that leadership is not about perfection but about presence. It is about showing up, every day, with an open heart and a willingness to serve the greater good. Trust in your own unique journey, and know that you are supported by the entire cosmic community as you step into this role. You are not alone—there are countless other Starseeds awakening to their own leadership, and together, you will help usher in a new era of light for humanity and the Earth.

Teaching and Guiding Others on the Ascension Path

As a Starseed leader, the call to teach and guide others on their spiritual journeys is a profound responsibility that requires both wisdom and empathy. It is not merely about imparting knowledge or facilitating the awakening of others, but about fostering a space where true transformation can occur. This process of mentorship is a delicate balance between offering guidance and allowing each individual to find their own unique path. The journey of ascension is intensely personal, and as a guide, you must learn to walk alongside those you serve, offering your light without overshadowing theirs.

To teach and guide others on the ascension path is to embody the role of both a spiritual mentor and a facilitator of higher consciousness. Your presence in this role becomes an energetic anchor, helping those around you to tap into their own potential while navigating the complexities of spiritual growth. There is a deep trust involved—both in the process of guiding and in the unfolding of each soul's journey. It is through this mutual trust that true spiritual evolution is nurtured.

Recognizing the Call to Teach

The call to teach is often subtle at first, manifesting as a quiet internal nudge or a recurring sense that you are meant to serve others in their spiritual awakening. You may find that people are drawn to you naturally, seeking advice, insights, or simply your calming presence. This is often the first sign that your energetic frequency is resonating at a level that can hold space for others. As your own connection to the Cosmic Flame deepens, so too does your capacity to guide others along the ascension path.

It is important to recognize that teaching and guiding others is not a linear process. Spiritual growth is a fluid, evolving journey, and your role as a guide will shift and transform over time. You may start by helping others awaken to their Starseed nature or introducing them to basic spiritual practices, but as you and those you guide continue to ascend, the work will become more nuanced and multidimensional. The ability to adapt to these shifts is a key aspect of effective spiritual teaching.

Your experiences on your own ascension journey, including the challenges you've faced and the lessons you've learned, become valuable tools in guiding others. Teaching is not about being perfect or all-knowing; it is about being open and authentic, willing to share your personal wisdom while also remaining a lifelong student of the universe.

Fostering Spiritual Autonomy

One of the most important aspects of guiding others on the ascension path is fostering spiritual autonomy. True spiritual growth occurs when individuals feel empowered to explore their own inner wisdom and connect with the divine in their own unique way. As a teacher, your role is not to dictate how others should navigate their spiritual journeys but to offer tools, insights, and support that help them discover their own path.

Encouraging spiritual autonomy begins with creating an open, non-judgmental space where individuals feel safe to express their beliefs, experiences, and challenges. The ascension journey can be an intense and sometimes isolating experience, and providing a space where people feel heard and understood is crucial for their growth. By holding this space, you help others build the confidence they need to trust their intuition and follow their inner guidance.

At the same time, it is essential to offer practical teachings that individuals can integrate into their daily lives. This includes spiritual practices such as meditation, energy work, and the use of sacred tools like crystals or sound healing. Providing a variety of techniques allows those you guide to experiment and discover what resonates with them. The goal is to empower them to take responsibility for their own spiritual evolution, rather than becoming dependent on external guidance.

Navigating the Complexities of Mentorship

The role of a spiritual guide is multifaceted and can present a number of challenges. It is important to remember that every soul is on its own unique journey, and the pace of each individual's growth will vary. Some may experience rapid awakening and transformation, while others may take a more gradual path. As a mentor, patience is key. It is not your role to push or rush anyone through their ascension process but to offer steady, compassionate support as they unfold at their own pace.

One of the challenges of teaching and guiding others is maintaining clear energetic boundaries. As you help others navigate their spiritual challenges, it is easy to absorb their emotional or energetic burdens. While empathy is a vital component of spiritual mentorship, it is crucial to develop techniques for protecting your own energy. Regularly connecting with the Cosmic Flame can help cleanse and rejuvenate your energy field, ensuring that you remain grounded and centered in your own frequency.

Additionally, there may be times when the individuals you guide encounter periods of resistance or setbacks. The ascension path is not always a smooth upward trajectory—it often involves confronting deep-seated fears, traumas, and karmic patterns that can create periods of stagnation or regression. As a guide, it is essential to offer reassurance during these times, helping individuals understand that these challenges are a natural part of the growth process. Your role is to help them see beyond the immediate struggle, recognizing it as an opportunity for profound healing and transformation.

The Art of Holding Space

One of the most valuable skills a Starseed leader can develop is the ability to hold space. This concept goes beyond simply being present with someone; it involves creating an energetic environment that supports deep spiritual work. Holding space means offering your full, non-judgmental attention and allowing others to express their thoughts, emotions, and spiritual experiences without fear of criticism or dismissal.

In a practical sense, holding space can take many forms. It might involve guiding someone through a meditation, listening as they process a spiritual breakthrough, or simply being present as they confront their inner shadows. The key is to offer this support without trying to fix or change the situation. Holding space is not about providing solutions but about creating a container where others can explore their inner world and come to their own insights.

When you hold space effectively, you serve as an energetic anchor. Your presence helps others feel safe as they navigate the often intense emotions and revelations that accompany spiritual awakening. This is particularly important during moments of deep transformation, when individuals may feel vulnerable or uncertain. By holding space with compassion and neutrality, you allow them to experience these moments fully, knowing that they are supported.

Teaching Through Example

Perhaps the most powerful way to teach and guide others is through your own example. The energy you carry, the way you live your life, and the choices you make all serve as a model for those around you. Spiritual teaching is not just about the words you speak or the practices you share; it is about embodying the principles of ascension in your everyday life.

As a Starseed leader, your actions speak louder than any spiritual lesson you might offer. How you handle challenges, how you interact with others, and how you maintain your connection to the Cosmic Flame all provide a living demonstration of what it means to walk the path of ascension. By being authentic and aligned in your own journey, you inspire others to do the same.

This does not mean you must be perfect or free from struggles. In fact, sharing your own challenges and how you navigate them can be one of the most powerful teaching tools. When others see that you too face difficulties but remain committed to your spiritual path, it offers them a sense of hope and motivation to continue on their own journey.

Building a Community of Learners

As you step into your role as a teacher and guide, you will naturally begin to attract a community of individuals who resonate with your energy and teachings. This community may take many forms—whether it is a small circle of close spiritual friends, a larger online following, or a formal group of students seeking guidance.

Creating and nurturing this community is a vital part of your role as a leader. It provides a space where individuals can support one another, share insights, and collectively raise their vibration. The energy of a community is powerful—when individuals come together with the shared intention of spiritual growth, they amplify each other's progress and create a ripple effect that extends far beyond the group itself.

As the leader of this community, your role is to hold the vision of ascension for the group. This means maintaining a clear focus on the higher purpose of the community and ensuring that the energy remains aligned with love, unity, and spiritual evolution. It also involves guiding group practices, such as meditations, discussions, or healing sessions, that support the collective growth of the group.

Ultimately, teaching and guiding others on the ascension path is a sacred service. It is an act of love and compassion that extends beyond the individual to touch the collective consciousness of humanity. By stepping into this role, you are not only facilitating the growth of those you guide but also contributing to the greater awakening of the planet. Your willingness to serve as a guide is a powerful force for transformation, helping to anchor the Cosmic Flame within the hearts of all those you encounter.

Leading Communities Through

Spiritual Transformation

As Starseeds step into leadership roles, one of the most powerful ways to effect change on both an individual and collective level is by guiding spiritual communities. Leading a community through spiritual transformation is more than organizing gatherings or sharing knowledge; it is about creating a safe, nurturing environment where collective energies can unite, amplify, and catalyze profound growth. In a time when humanity is awakening en masse, leaders who can facilitate these transformational spaces hold the key to anchoring higher frequencies on Earth, helping humanity ascend into a new phase of consciousness.

Spiritual communities, whether they take the form of in-person groups, online forums, or global networks, are beacons of light in a world that is rapidly evolving. As a Starseed leader, your role is to help these communities not only survive the chaotic changes that come with awakening but thrive through them. This is a sacred duty, one that calls for empathy, vision, and a deep understanding of the ascension process. The individuals within your community are undergoing their own unique journeys, and as a leader, your task is to guide them toward unity, collective healing, and spiritual ascension.

The Power of Community in Spiritual Growth

A community creates a container for collective energy. In spiritual terms, this collective energy is greater than the sum of its parts. When individuals come together with a shared intention of growth, healing, and ascension, their combined frequency generates a powerful field of transformation. In such spaces, each person's journey is supported, amplified, and accelerated by the energies of others. This is the true magic of community—the way it holds space for the collective consciousness to rise, while still honoring the individuality of each member's path.

For many Starseeds, spiritual communities offer something they have long been seeking: connection. Many who walk the ascension path feel isolated, misunderstood, or disconnected from the world around them. They may struggle with the intensity of their awakening, feeling as though they are alone in their experiences. Spiritual communities provide a sanctuary, a place where like-minded souls can come together, share their struggles, celebrate their breakthroughs, and support one another through the ups and downs of the spiritual journey.

However, leading such a community requires more than just gathering people together. It requires an understanding of group dynamics, the ability to hold space for diverse perspectives, and the vision to guide the community through both the practical and spiritual challenges that will inevitably arise. As a leader, your energy will set the tone for the group, so it is crucial that you remain grounded, centered, and connected to your own spiritual path.

Cultivating a High-Vibration Community

One of the primary responsibilities of a Starseed leader is to maintain the energetic integrity of the community. This means cultivating a high-vibration environment where love, unity, and compassion are the guiding principles. Every member of the community will bring their own energy, and as a leader, it is your task to ensure that the collective frequency remains aligned with the higher goals of spiritual transformation.

This can be achieved in several ways. First and foremost, it is essential to set a clear intention for the community. Whether your community is focused on healing, ascension practices, or spiritual exploration, having a shared purpose helps to create coherence within the group. This intention acts as a spiritual anchor, guiding the group's energy and keeping it focused on the path of growth and evolution.

Secondly, fostering a sense of openness and inclusion is critical. In any spiritual community, there will be individuals at different stages of their journey. Some may be just beginning their awakening, while others may be more advanced in their spiritual development. It is important to create an environment where all voices are heard, respected, and valued. Encouraging each member to share their insights, experiences, and challenges not only strengthens the community but also creates a space where everyone feels they are contributing to the collective ascension.

Additionally, maintaining a high-vibration community means addressing any conflicts or negative energies that may arise. As with any group of people, there will be moments when misunderstandings or energetic imbalances occur. It is important to approach these situations with compassion and clarity, addressing issues as they arise without allowing them to disrupt the harmony of the group. The energy of the community should always be one of love, respect, and mutual support.

Leadership Through Service

Leading a spiritual community is not about being in control or having all the answers; it is about serving those who are on their own unique spiritual journeys. This requires a deep sense of humility and a commitment to placing the needs of the community above your own egoic desires. Leadership through service means being attuned to the collective energy of the group, listening to the needs of its members, and offering guidance that supports their highest good.

In practice, this might involve facilitating group meditations, guiding discussions, or organizing events that help the community stay connected to its spiritual goals. It could also mean offering individual support to members who are going through difficult times in their spiritual journeys, providing a listening ear or offering energy healing when needed. As a leader, you are both a guide and a servant, helping to create a space where the community can flourish.

One of the greatest gifts you can offer your community is your own authentic presence. By being open, vulnerable, and true to yourself, you create a space where others feel safe to do the same. When members of the community see you navigating your own spiritual challenges with grace and humility, they are inspired to approach their own growth in a similar way. Leading by example is one of the most powerful tools you have as a Starseed leader.

Building Ritual and Tradition

Rituals and traditions play a significant role in fostering unity and coherence within a spiritual community. These practices create a sense of continuity and shared experience, helping to anchor the group's energy and keep it focused on its higher purpose. As a leader, you have the opportunity to create rituals that resonate with the unique energy of your community, drawing on both ancient traditions and new spiritual practices that align with the group's collective intention.

These rituals can take many forms, from group meditations and energy healing sessions to seasonal celebrations or moon gatherings. The key is to create practices that are meaningful to the group and that help to reinforce the community's connection to the Cosmic Flame and the larger ascension process. By incorporating ritual into your community, you provide members with a way to deepen their spiritual practice and strengthen their connection to the collective energy.

Tradition, in this sense, does not have to be rigid or dogmatic. Instead, it is about creating shared experiences that help the community stay grounded in its spiritual purpose. These traditions can evolve as the community grows, adapting to the changing needs and energies of the group. The goal is to create a rhythm of practice that supports the ongoing transformation of the community, helping its members stay aligned with their highest selves.

Anchoring Collective Ascension

The true power of a spiritual community lies in its ability to anchor higher frequencies on Earth. When individuals come together with the shared goal of ascension, their collective energy has a profound impact on the planet. As a Starseed leader, your community becomes a microcosm of the larger ascension process. By guiding your group through its own spiritual transformation, you are also contributing to the global shift in consciousness.

This work is both spiritual and practical. On a spiritual level, your community serves as a beacon of light, holding space for the higher frequencies of the Cosmic Flame to anchor on Earth. Through group practices, meditations, and rituals, the collective energy of the community becomes a force for planetary healing and transformation. As your community grows in strength and coherence, its impact on the larger world becomes more profound.

On a practical level, your community can also play a role in social transformation. By embodying the principles of love, unity, and compassion, your group becomes a model for how humanity can live in alignment with higher consciousness. This might involve engaging in community service, environmental initiatives, or other actions that help to elevate the collective energy of the planet. In this way, your community is not only contributing to its own ascension but also to the ascension of the world around it.

The Sacred Duty of Leadership

Leading a spiritual community through transformation is a sacred duty, one that requires deep commitment, compassion, and vision. It is a role that asks you to hold space for the growth of others while also staying deeply connected to your own spiritual path. As a Starseed leader, you are both a guide and a servant, helping to facilitate the awakening of those around you while contributing to the larger ascension of humanity.

Through your leadership, you create a space where individuals can come together, support one another, and collectively raise their vibration. You offer your community the tools, guidance, and energetic support it needs to navigate the challenges of ascension, while also providing a vision of what is possible when we come together in unity and love.

In this work, you are not alone. The energy of the Cosmic Flame flows through you, guiding and supporting you as you guide others. By stepping into your role as a leader, you become a conduit for this divine energy, helping to anchor it on Earth and assist in the transformation of the planet. This is the true power of community—when we come together in the light of the Cosmic Flame, we become a force for profound, lasting change.

Advanced Cosmic Leadership and Global Ascension Mastery

In the vast tapestry of human and cosmic evolution, few roles hold as much transformative power as that of the advanced cosmic leader. As a Starseed who has journeyed through the personal realms of awakening, growth, and spiritual expansion, stepping into the advanced realm of cosmic leadership is both a sacred responsibility and a profound calling. At this level, leadership is no longer about guiding individuals or even small communities through spiritual transformation; it is about inspiring, uplifting, and leading humanity—and beyond—toward collective ascension.

The essence of advanced cosmic leadership lies in the ability to channel higher-dimensional wisdom, activate planetary healing, and catalyze large-scale shifts in consciousness. Those who feel called to this path must first recognize that their work extends far beyond themselves. Advanced cosmic leaders operate on a multidimensional scale, serving not only the physical plane but also the subtle, energetic grids that connect Earth to the cosmos. They become conduits of divine energy, capable of orchestrating global meditations, directing celestial energies, and anchoring the Cosmic Flame into Earth's energetic field to elevate the collective frequency of all beings.

Understanding the Role of a Cosmic Leader

The advanced cosmic leader holds a unique position within the grand framework of ascension. Unlike traditional leadership, which often focuses on hierarchical structures, cosmic leadership is about harmonizing with the higher frequencies of the universe and helping others do the same. It is the art of being both a guide and a vessel for divine energy, with the ultimate goal of unifying human consciousness with that of the cosmos.

At its core, cosmic leadership is a service to the collective. It requires a profound shift from ego-based leadership, which centers on individual success, to soul-based leadership, which centers on planetary and cosmic evolution. This form of leadership is rooted in the understanding that Earth's ascension is intrinsically connected to the broader ascension of the cosmos. Every thought, action, and vibration of the leader influences the greater energy matrix, affecting not only those within their immediate circle but also the entire planetary field.

An advanced cosmic leader is someone who has already mastered the foundational practices of personal ascension, healing, and energy work. They understand the intricate workings of the Cosmic Flame, the energetic grid of Earth, and the multidimensional realms that govern spiritual evolution. They also possess a deep connection to higher-dimensional beings, galactic councils, and cosmic guides, receiving direct wisdom and insight from these higher sources. This wisdom allows them to navigate the complexities of global ascension with grace, clarity, and precision.

Leading Mass Spiritual Movements

One of the most significant roles of an advanced cosmic leader is to inspire and lead mass spiritual movements. These movements are vital in anchoring higher frequencies on Earth, facilitating collective healing, and accelerating humanity's evolution toward a more unified and enlightened state of consciousness. Unlike smaller spiritual communities, mass movements require a more expansive vision, one that transcends individual or local concerns and taps into the global consciousness.

Leading such movements begins with setting a clear and powerful intention. This intention must resonate not only with those who are spiritually inclined but also with the larger energy field of the planet. Cosmic leaders must be adept at tuning into the collective consciousness, understanding its needs, challenges, and potential, and then guiding that energy toward transformation. By holding a clear vision for global ascension and anchoring it through rituals, meditations, and collective practices, the leader creates a resonance that others can align with, allowing the movement to grow organically and energetically.

To inspire mass spiritual movements, advanced cosmic leaders often work closely with galactic guides and higher councils to channel messages of hope, unity, and love to the world. These messages serve as energetic blueprints that awaken dormant codes within humanity, activating a desire for change and transformation. Cosmic leaders then provide practical tools, such as group meditations, planetary healing rituals, and energy grids, to ground these higher energies into the physical realm.

A key aspect of leading mass movements is the ability to remain grounded amidst the powerful energies being activated. Cosmic leaders must be deeply rooted in their own practices, ensuring that their physical, emotional, and energetic bodies are capable of handling the immense flows of energy they will be channeling. This requires ongoing self-care, energy work, and connection to the Cosmic Flame to maintain balance and prevent burnout.

Global Meditations and Planetary Healing

One of the most effective tools for advanced cosmic leadership is the practice of global meditation. These meditations act as a bridge between individual consciousness and the collective field, allowing large groups of people to align their intentions, energy, and frequency toward a shared goal of planetary healing and ascension. When guided by a cosmic leader, global meditations can generate profound shifts in Earth's energetic field, helping to stabilize and elevate the planet's frequency.

The power of global meditation lies in its ability to harness collective energy. When individuals across the world meditate with the same intention, their combined energy creates a powerful resonance that ripples through the collective consciousness. Cosmic leaders understand how to direct this energy toward specific areas of need, whether it be healing Earth's energetic grid, clearing negative frequencies from the planet's aura, or anchoring higher-dimensional light codes into the physical realm.

In leading global meditations, cosmic leaders often work with sacred geometry, light language, and sound frequencies to amplify the effects of the practice. These tools help to create an energetic template that holds the intention of the meditation, allowing it to manifest more powerfully in the physical world. By incorporating these advanced techniques, cosmic leaders can guide meditations that not only heal individuals but also contribute to the overall ascension of the planet.

Another vital aspect of planetary healing is working with Earth's energy grids. Advanced cosmic leaders have a deep understanding of these grids and how they interact with the Cosmic Flame. They know how to tap into these grids to anchor light codes, transmute lower energies, and stabilize the planet during times of upheaval. By working with these grids in conjunction with global meditations, cosmic leaders can help accelerate Earth's healing and ascension process.

Anchoring the Cosmic Flame for Global Ascension

Perhaps the most significant role of an advanced cosmic leader is to anchor the Cosmic Flame into the planetary field, facilitating global ascension. The Cosmic Flame is a powerful force of transformation, capable of transmuting lower energies, activating higher consciousness, and unifying human souls with the divine. Cosmic leaders serve as conduits for this flame, allowing it to flow through them and into the collective consciousness.

Anchoring the Cosmic Flame requires advanced energy work, deep spiritual alignment, and a profound connection to the higher realms. Cosmic leaders must be able to hold the frequency of the Cosmic Flame within their own energy field while simultaneously directing it toward the planet. This is no small task, as the intensity of the flame can be overwhelming for those who are not fully prepared. However, for those who have mastered the necessary practices, the Cosmic Flame becomes a tool of profound transformation, capable of igniting global shifts in consciousness.

To effectively anchor the Cosmic Flame, cosmic leaders often work with advanced rituals, sacred sites, and planetary energy grids. By channeling the flame into these powerful energy points, they can magnify its effects, allowing it to spread more quickly and effectively across the planet. This process helps to elevate Earth's vibration, clear negative energies, and activate higher-dimensional light codes that accelerate the ascension process.

Embodying the Cosmic Leader Archetype

Advanced cosmic leadership is not merely a role; it is an archetype, a sacred embodiment of divine wisdom, love, and service. To fully step into this archetype, cosmic leaders must integrate all aspects of their being—physical, emotional, mental, and spiritual—into a harmonious whole. They must transcend the limitations of the ego, align with their soul's higher purpose, and commit to serving the collective with compassion, humility, and grace.

As a cosmic leader, you become a living embodiment of the Cosmic Flame, a beacon of light for others to follow. Your actions, thoughts, and energy ripple out into the world, influencing the collective consciousness and guiding humanity toward its highest potential. Through your leadership, you hold the power to inspire mass movements, heal the planet, and catalyze the global ascension process.

In this sacred role, you are never alone. You are supported by the energies of the cosmos, the guidance of higher-dimensional beings, and the collective power of all those who walk the path of ascension with you. Together, you create a unified field of consciousness, one that holds the potential for profound transformation and the ultimate realization of humanity's divine destiny.

In your hands, the Cosmic Flame becomes a tool of global healing, a force for planetary evolution, and a beacon of hope for all souls seeking the light. As an advanced cosmic leader, your work is not just for today but for the future of all humanity, guiding the world into an era of unity, peace, and ascended consciousness. The time is now to embrace your role, ignite the Cosmic Flame, and lead the way into the new paradigm of global ascension.

THE END

Printed in Great Britain
by Amazon

db79995f-60ba-4d99-b0a7-3fd319edcf74R01